Historical American Biographies

JOHN MUIR
Crusader for the Wilderness

Karen Clemens Warrick

Enslow Publishers, Inc.

40 Industrial Road   PO Box 38
Box 398   Aldershot
Berkeley Heights, NJ 07922   Hants GU12 6BP
USA   UK

http://www.enslow.com

Acknowledgments

Special thanks to the members of my critique group who never failed to encourage me to make my writing the best it could be and therefore worthy of John Muir's story.

Copyright © 2002 by Karen Clemens Warrick

Library of Congress Cataloging-in-Publication Data

Warrick, Karen Clemens.
    John Muir: crusader for the wilderness / Karen Clemens Warrick.
      p. cm. - (Historical American biographies)
    Includes bibliographical references (p.).
    Summary: Describes the life of the naturalist who became a founder of the Sierra Club and a proponent of the establishment of national parks in America.
    ISBN 0-7660-1622-6
    1. Muir, John, 1838–1914. 2. Conservationist—United States—Juvenile literature. 3. Naturalists—United States-Juvenile literature. [1. Muir, John, 1838–1914. 2. Conservationists. 3. Naturalists.] I. Title. II. Series.
    QH31.M9 W37 2001
    333.7'2'092-dc21

                                   2001003000

Printed in the United States of America

10 9 8 7 6 5 4 3 2 1

To Our Readers: We have done our best to make sure all Internet addresses in this book were active and appropriate when we went to press. However, the author and the publisher have no control over and assume no liability for the material available on those Internet sites or on other Web sites they may link to. Any comments or suggestions can be sent by e-mail to comments@enslow.com or to the address on the back cover.

Illustration Credits: Courtesy of Kevin Berry, p. 50; Courtesy Sierra Club, reproduced from the *Dictionary of American Portraits*, published by Dover Publications, Inc., in 1967, p.4; Dorothy Clemens, p. 62; Enslow Publishers, Inc., pp. 46, 67, 84; Erie Canal Museum, p. 22; John Muir National Historic Site, pp. 113, 114; John Muir Papers, Holt-Atherton Department of Special Collections, University of the Pacific Libraries, © 1984 Muir-Hanna Trust, pp. 12, 14, 40, 70, 82, 105; Karen Clemens Warrick, pp. 8, 68, 75; State Historical Society of Wisconsin, Whi (D487) 9783, p. 35; State Historical Society of Wisconsin, Whi (X32) 8764, p. 37; Yosemite National Park, pp. 91, 98.

Cover Illustration: © Corel Corporation (Background); Courtesy Sierra Club, reproduced from the *Dictionary of American Portraits*, published by Dover Publications, Inc., in 1967 (Muir Portrait).

CONTENTS

John Muir

1

"AN ADVENTURE WITH A DOG AND A GLACIER"

I t was already late when John Muir and his companion, a little dog named Stickeen, headed back to camp on the shore of Alaska's Taylor Bay. The rain was threatening to turn to snow and Muir did not want to be caught after dark in a blizzard on the glacier, a vast river of ice.[1] Muir and Stickeen had set out before dawn and spent hours working their way up the ice-filled canyon. Now he took the most direct route back, across unexplored ice. A network of crevasses, or deep canyons, crisscrossed his path. Muir jumped those that were narrow enough and Stickeen followed bravely.

Soon Muir found his way barred by a crevasse so wide that he preferred not to jump it. He ran along its edge for a mile, looking for a safer way across but did not find one. He and Stickeen had to jump. They made it with only inches to spare. Muir and Stickeen hurried on, hoping the worst was behind them.[2] But after traveling only a few more yards, they came to the edge of an even wider crevasse. After a brief exploration, Muir discovered that they were trapped. The only escape route was "an almost inaccessible sliver [or ice] bridge."[3]

This ice bridge was only a few inches wide. Its top had weathered to a knife-sharp edge. It stretched about seventy feet from one side of the crevasse to the other. The middle section of the bridge dipped twenty-five to thirty feet below the glacier's surface. The ends were attached to opposite sides of the crevasse about eight or ten feet below the brink. Getting down the almost vertical walls to the bridge and up the other side would be a challenge.

Muir went to work. Leaning over the edge, he used his axe to cut a step about eighteen inches from the top. Then, balancing on that step, he lowered himself cautiously over the edge. As Muir held on with his left hand, he reached down and cut another step below the first one, then another, and another, until he reached the level of the sliver-bridge.

Stickeen seemed to understand what was planned. As Muir chipped away, the little dog looked down into the crevasse. He studied the narrow, dangerous, escape route and began to cry.[4] He took one more look, then ran off, looking for another way to cross.

By now, Muir had cut a level platform six or eight inches wide at the end of the bridge. Balanced on this slippery little platform, he stooped, straddled the ice sliver, and tried to ignore "the tremendous abyss."[5] He shaved off the knife-sharp edge right in front of him. Then he slid carefully forward, his knees pressed against the sides of the bridge. By repeating this process again and again, Muir traveled the seventy feet across the crevasse.

When he reached the other side, Muir later wrote, he faced "the most trying part of the adventure. [He had to stand up to cut] a step-ladder in the nearly vertical face of the wall—chipping, climbing, holding on with feet and fingers in mere notches."[6]

By the time Muir reached the top safely, Stickeen was back, but still on the other side of the crevasse. Frantically, the dog raced back and forth, howling.

Muir coaxed and encouraged his companion to cross the ice bridge. When that did not work, he pretended to leave the little dog behind. Finally,

Stickeen approached the edge. Muir's own words best describe what happened next:

> He [Stickeen] pressed his body against the ice as if trying to get the advantage of friction of every hair, gazed at the first step, put his little feet together and slid them slowly, slowly over the edge and down onto it, bunching all four up, almost standing on his head. Then without lifting his feet . . . he slowly worked them over the edge of the step and down into the next one . . . until he gained the bridge.[7]

Stickeen carefully set one foot down, then the next, as he made his way across the narrow sliver. Muir got down on his knees and leaned over the

John Muir and Stickeen worked their way up an ice-filled canyon much like this tide-water glacier that flows into Glacier Bay today.

Stickeen

After their adventure, John Muir never saw Stickeen again, but the little dog had made an impression on him. Muir worked seventeen years on Stickeen's story. In 1897, he sent the manuscript to *Century Magazine*, claiming it had cost him more time and effort than anything else he had ever written. It was published under the title "An Adventure with a Dog and a Glacier." In 1909, it was republished as a book, and simply called *Stickeen*. The book brought Muir more fan mail than anything else he ever wrote.[8]

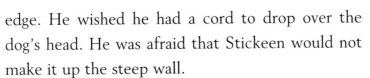

edge. He wished he had a cord to drop over the dog's head. He was afraid that Stickeen would not make it up the steep wall.

The dog stopped when he reached the wall. Even years later, Muir remembered how he studied "the notched steps and finger holds . . . as if counting them and fixing the position of each . . . Then suddenly up he came in a springy rush . . . so quickly that [I] could not see how it was done."[9]

Muir tried to catch Stickeen and pet him, but the little dog went wild. Muir paints this vivid picture:

> He flashed and darted hither and thither . . . swirling round and round in giddy loops and circles like a leaf in a whirlwind, lying down and rolling over and over,

sideways and heels over head . . . [then] he flashed
off two or three hundred yards . . . turning suddenly,
came back in [a] wild rush and launched himself at
my face, almost knocking me down. All the time
screeching and screaming and shouting as if saying,
"Saved! saved! saved!"[10]

The two companions made it back to camp
about ten o'clock that night without any other trials.
For the rest of the trip, when all was quiet about the
campfire, Stickeen would rest his head on Muir's
knee, and give him a look of undying devotion.

2

SCOTTISH CASTLES AND BAIRNS

J ohn Muir was an adventure-loving boy even as a "wee bairn" (child) growing up in Dunbar, Scotland, a fishing village along the North Sea which separates the British Isles from Europe. He often disobeyed the strict orders of his father, Daniel Muir, and scaled the garden wall to explore the countryside with his friends. The boys' favorite playground was Dunbar Castle, which was already one thousand years old in the 1840s. Inside its crumbling walls and towers they played a game called "scootchers." One boy would attempt an adventure, then dare the others to do the same.

At first, it was exciting enough to touch the bones of prisoners who had died long ago. Then

John's mother, Ann Gilrye Muir, also loved nature.

the boys discovered a room deep beneath the castle. The ceiling had fallen into a pit so deep the boys could not see the floor below. Only nine-year-old John was daring enough to brave the dark. Digging his fingers and toes into cracks, he lowered himself down the rock wall. Finally, he reached the bottom and stood for a moment to rest his shaking muscles. The light seemed far away when he looked up to where the others waited. It took all his strength to reach the top. His friends voted this the best scootcher of all.[1] None of them dared go down into that pit. Having won the game, John hurried home to the thrashing his father was sure to give him for breaking the rules again.

The Muir Family

Little is known about the childhood of Daniel Muir, John's father. His parents, John and Sarah Higgs Muir, had died when he was only a year old. After that, Daniel and Mary, his twelve-year-old sister, lived on a farm that belonged to relatives. Daniel was a bright, handsome boy who enjoyed athletic games and loved to sing. He even made himself a

Wild Muir

Grandfather David Gilrye took John on his first ventures into the countryside when he was only three. He encouraged his grandson to use his eyes and ears to read the world around him. Muir remembered making a wonderful discovery on one of these walks. The two had sat down to rest on a haystack when John heard "a sharp, prickly stinging cry."[2] He dug into the hay and soon discovered the source of the strange sound–a mother field mouse with six babies. From that time on, John was fascinated by the wonders of the natural world.

John's escapes to the countryside were the best times of his young life, even though he was often spanked for disobedience.[3] Roaming free among the hills, fields, and marshland of Scotland, he felt "wild."[4] Wildness—in this sense—later became a way of life for John Muir.

This portrait of John's father Daniel Muir was painted from memory by his daughter Mary Muir Hand after his death in 1885.

violin, then ran ten miles through mud and rain to get strings for it.[5] "While yet more boy than man," Daniel Muir joined the British Army and was sent to Dunbar, Scotland, as a recruiting sergeant.[6] It was his duty to enlist other young men in the army. He soon married a young woman who had inherited a grain-and-food store. After paying for his release from the army (an option for officers who wished to leave the army before serving all their time), the young man settled down to manage his wife's business. Daniel had one child with his first wife, but their life together was brief. His wife and child died, leaving him alone again.

Ann Gilrye lived with her parents in a house across the street from Muir's business. The twenty-year-old woman wrote poetry, painted landscapes, and loved long walks in the countryside. Daniel Muir soon became a frequent visitor to her home. Ann's parents, however, did not want her to marry

Muir. They thought his religious beliefs were too strict. Daniel and the Gilryes attended the community Presbyterian Church. Muir often criticized church members because they were not always praying and shouting to the Lord. However, the Gilryes' daughter was strong-willed and in love. On November 28, 1833, Ann became Daniel Muir's second wife.

Daniel and Ann Muir had eight children. Their first daughter, Margaret, was born in 1834. Sarah arrived in 1836, and John was born on April 21, 1838. Two years later, David was born, then Daniel, Jr., in 1843. Twin sisters, Mary and Annie, were added to the family in 1846. Joanna, the Muirs' last child, was born in 1850.

John's birthplace was a three-story stone house. The family lived in the two upper floors above his father's grain and produce business. The rooms were unnaturally gloomy. Some of the windows had been boarded up to reduce taxes that were collected for each window, a common way to assess property taxes at that time.

The family would begin each day with oatmeal porridge and a little milk for breakfast. The small portions could be eaten in a few minutes, but none of the children dreamed of asking for more because Daniel Muir believed a frugal diet was good for the soul. The noon meal was usually vegetable broth, and maybe a small piece of boiled mutton, and barley scones—biscuits that John hated.[7] He ate them anyway to try to fill himself up. For afternoon tea, the Muir children had content, a drink made by adding a little milk and sugar to water, half a slice of bread without butter, and more scones. The evening meal was a boiled potato and still more scones.

John's "first conscious memory" was hearing the old Scottish songs played by Daniel Muir on his handmade violin.[8] However, by the time John was five or six, his father had joined a new church organization, the Disciples of Christ. This group wished to live by the simple ways of the primitive church, as it was believed to have been during Christ's days on earth. From then on, Daniel Muir only allowed hymn-singing. He banned pictures from the walls. No one was permitted to talk or laugh while they ate, because each meal was regarded as a gift from God. Daniel Muir was considered a religious fanatic, even by his most devout neighbors.

Ann Muir did her best to make her children's life bearable. She expressed her thoughts and feelings by signals that her seven children quickly learned to read. A small, fleeting smile told them when she thought their father was being ridiculous. A slightly raised eyebrow or a quick frown said, "I think he's wrong."[9]

When necessary, Ann Muir quietly defended the children from their father. There were many times she hurried John into bed before his father could give him a thrashing. Whippings were a common form of punishment, and like most Scottish fathers in those days, Daniel Muir expected to be obeyed. However, the children and their mother managed to make life tolerable for themselves by sticking together.

John shared a love of nature with his mother. She taught him to enjoy small pleasures whenever he had the chance.[10] It was his mother and her

Another Daring Scootcher

Both of John's parents tried to discourage his adventurous spirit, but with little success. One night while playing scootchers with his brother David, John climbed out the window of their third-story bedroom. He held onto the sill with one hand and dangled over the edge of the slate roof. When David matched his dare, John climbed up the slates to the top of the roof. He straddled the roof and let the wind fill his nightshirt like a sail. David slipped as he tried to match his brother's dare. John had to grab David by the feet and pull him back inside the window. Both boys almost fell off the roof.

A half-century later, Muir revisited his childhood home. After examining the slickness of the slates and the pitch of the roof, he exclaimed that even with all his mountaineering experience, "what [he] had done in daring boyhood was now beyond [his] skill."[11]

parents, David and Margaret Gilrye, who taught John to give and receive love.

School Days

When John entered the Dunbar primary school at the age of three, he could already read. Grandfather Gilrye had taught him letters and words from signs they saw during walks along the streets of Dunbar. Grandfather also taught his grandson his numbers using the town's tower clock, a mechanical marvel John never forgot.

Even though the lessons were easy for him, John hated school.[12] Boys were whipped to make sure they memorized their spelling words and arithmetic rules. Lessons in English, French and Latin grammar, history, and geography were beaten into them. "The Scotch [Scots]," Muir said later, ". . . made the discovery that there was a connection between the skin and the memory. The whole educational system was founded on leather."[13]

John thought all the memorization was boring. In addition to schoolwork, Daniel Muir made his son learn hymns and Bible verses every day. By the time John was ten, he had memorized all of the New Testament and part of the Old.

The only parts of school that excited John were natural history lessons, especially those about the New World. He was impressed by Scottish ornithologist Alexander Wilson's descriptions of the fish hawk and the bald eagle, which he had observed during years spent in the wilds of North America. The schoolboy was also fascinated by naturalist John Audubon's wonderful illustrated stories of American birds. In another lesson, John read about trees found in the American forests. The most interesting one described was the sugar maple. Then in 1848, news reached Dunbar that gold had been discovered in a United States territory called California. Gold was said to be so plentiful that men were finding it by the bucketful. America now seemed even more wonderful to ten-year-old John and his schoolmates.[14]

A New World

Every evening, John and David ran across the street to study in the friendly warmth of the Gilrye living room. After their Grandfather heard them recite lessons, Grandmother gave them tea and goodies. They were studying as usual on February 18, 1849, when Daniel Muir interrupted, "Bairns," he said, "you need [not] learn your lessons [tonight], for we're [going] to America [in] the morn!"[15] Fifty-eight years later, John Muir still remembered his delighted reaction: "No more grammar, but boundless woods full of mysterious good things; trees full of sugar, growing in ground full of gold; hawks, eagles . . . filling the sky; millions of birds' nests . . . "[16]

After Daniel Muir left the room, Grandfather Gilrye gave each boy a gold coin for a keepsake. He looked very serious when he said, "in a low, trembling, troubled voice, 'Ah, poor laddies, you'll find something else ower the sea [besides] gold and sugar, birds' nests and freedom [from] lessons and schools. You'll find plenty hard, hard work.'"[17]

None of the treasures that John imagined had attracted his father to America. Daniel Muir wanted to follow the teachings of the Disciples of Christ and live in a simple manner. Ann Muir had not been consulted about the move. Her husband had simply told her she must leave her home and parents. Being the dutiful wife, Ann began to pack without a complaint. However, Grandfather Gilrye did not accept the decision so easily. He insisted that Ann Muir and the youngest children should stay in Dunbar until Daniel had found a place for the family to live in America. Fifteen-year-old Margaret stayed to help her mother take care of six-year-old Daniel, Jr., and the two-year-old twins, Annie and Mary.

So the next morning, Daniel, Sarah, David, and John Muir went by rail to Glasgow, "and then sailed joyfully away from beloved Scotland," John wrote years later. "We were too young and full of hope for fear or regret . . . Even [the idea of] . . . leaving

Grandparents . . . mother, sisters, and brother [behind] was quickly quenched in young joy."[18]

Their voyage on the old-fashioned sailing vessel took six weeks and three days. Daniel Muir and Sarah were seasick most of the time. John and David, left on their own, spent every day on deck. They learned the names of all the ropes and sails. The ship's crew pointed out whales, dolphins, and seabirds and told the boys stories about these wonderful creatures. John especially loved the storms, when great waves smashed against the bow and made the whole ship shudder.[19]

When he was able to leave his cabin, Daniel Muir gave his sons some candy their mother had sent along, then paid little attention to them. He was too busy with prayer meetings or gathering information about their new homeland.

The Muirs landed at New York on April 5, 1849. After being cleared through the Staten Island quarantine station (where immigrants were examined for infectious diseases and other conditions that would prevent them from working), the family gathered their belongings and ventured into the new world—America.

A team of three mules pulls an Erie-Canal packet boat (near the center of the picture).

3

A WHOLE
NEW WORLD

Daniel Muir booked passage for himself and the three children up the Hudson River to Albany, New York, where their baggage was transferred to an Erie-Canal boat that took them to Buffalo. Then they traveled through Lakes Erie, Huron, and Michigan to Milwaukee, Wisconsin.

Within two weeks, Daniel Muir filed a homestead claim on eighty acres near Portage, Wisconsin, and built an open-faced cabin on a rise over looking a lake. He named their new farm "Fountain Lake" for its many springs. American Indians had given up their claim to the lands northwest of Fountain Lake only a year before in May 1848, when Wisconsin became a state. The Muirs' nearest neighbor lived

The Erie Canal

In 1825, the Erie Canal opened and became a major factor in attracting settlers like the Muirs to the Midwest. The canal made it possible to go from New York City to ports on Lake Michigan's western shore by an all-water route, which was much easier than overland travel. The lightweight packet boats were pulled by horses that trotted along the towpath, a road on the canal's bank. The boats could make the 547-kilometer trip (about 340 miles) between the Hudson River and Buffalo in three-and-a-half days. The Erie Canal was considered the engineering wonder of its time.

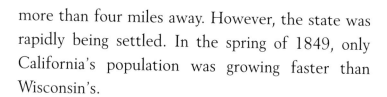

more than four miles away. However, the state was rapidly being settled. In the spring of 1849, only California's population was growing faster than Wisconsin's.

A Wilderness Home

The Muir children first saw the new family farm in May 1849. The rolling, tree-covered hills seemed like a wilderness paradise to eleven-year-old John. Even before the wagon stopped, he spotted a bird's nest filled with eggs. Ignoring the screaming protests of the parent blue jays, John and David climbed the tree for a closer look.

The farm was home to many birds and other animals. John learned to recognize hawks, owls, bobwhites, prairie chickens, and ruffed grouse. He discovered bats, squirrels, chipmunks, rabbits, muskrats, and snapping turtles. One summer evening, John was amazed by thousands of tiny glowing lights in the meadow—blinking off and on. The hired man showed the boys how to catch the flickering insects, called lightning bugs or fireflies.

Wisconsin thunderstorms, too, fascinated John. He watched as dark clouds rolled across the sky, dropping hail and rain. Several times, the boys saw trees shattered by lightning. Years later, Muir wrote, "Here without knowing it we still were at school; every wild lesson a love lesson, not whipped but charmed into us . . . how utterly happy it made us."[1]

During the first summer, John's only regular job was to help Sarah with the laundry. Every Monday, they carried water from a spring, heated it on an open fire, soaped the clothes in a wooden tub, wrung out the water, and then hung the clothes to dry. When this backbreaking task was finished, the children were free to explore.

In November, when the new eight-room house was finished, Ann Muir, Margaret, Daniel Jr., Annie, and Mary arrived. The entire family was together again, ready to build a new life in America.

"Hard, Hard Work"

In the spring of 1850, Grandfather Gilrye's prediction came true. John's days of freedom were replaced by hard work. As the oldest boy, he was given the toughest job—plowing the fields that had been cleared the year before. Only twelve years old, John had to reach up to grasp the plow's handles and fight to keep it upright. He needed his brother David's help to turn the plow at the end of each furrow. Many times, John wanted to quit, but he knew his father would beat him if he did.[2] By the end of each day, he could hardly stay awake during family prayers.

John's summer chore was hoeing the fields he had plowed. David, Margaret, and Sarah helped. Daniel Muir assigned each child a different row, so they would not waste time talking. All day long the children's hoes rose and fell. They could not even stop for a drink of water. Their father would thrash them for leaving their work. With the little free time they did have during the summer, John and David built a plank boat. They rowed around the lake and learned to swim underwater by imitating frogs.

In winter, Wisconsin temperatures often fell below zero. The stove in the Muirs' kitchen was the only heat for the entire house, and Daniel Muir refused to keep the fire burning at night. He did not want time wasted on cutting and carrying extra wood. So the house was very cold each morning when the family woke at six. Everyone stood around the cold stove and shivered. What was even worse, John later wrote, "beneath [the stove] we found our socks and coarse soggy boots frozen solid. We were not allowed to start even [a] little fire . . . to thaw them."[3] Instead, they were expected to put the stiff, cold shoes on and go out to feed the horses and cattle, grind axes, and bring in wood for a fire to cook breakfast. No matter what the weather, there was always something to do: shelling corn, making ax handles or ox-yokes, or mending things.

For a while, Daniel Muir decided his family should not eat meat and only needed one meal a day. John complained about the unhealthy diet, citing Bible passages to support his arguments. Daniel finally allowed the family to eat meat again.

All the Muir children, except Joanna, the baby born in 1850 at Fountain Lake Farm, worked like slaves. "Even when sick," John wrote, "we were held to our tasks. . . . Once in harvest-time I had the mumps and was unable to swallow any food except milk, but this was not allowed to make any difference."[4]

While his family worked, Daniel Muir spent most of his time studying the Bible. On Sundays he would deliver sermons in any Christian church that would have him. When he rode off to preach in

The Story of My Boyhood and Youth

When they first settled at Fountain Lake Farm, Daniel Muir bought the boys a horse named Jack. Each evening, John and David rode Jack to bring in the cows. However, if the boys were a few minutes late, Jack got in the habit of going by himself to fetch the cows. It made Daniel Muir angry to see the horse chasing the cows and making them run.[5] One evening after this happened, his father ordered John to shoot the horse. Daniel changed his mind, but the horse was sold to a man headed for the California gold fields, and the boys lost a favorite pet.

One hot summer day, Daniel Muir drove Nob, the family's favorite buggy horse, twenty-four miles over sandy roads so he would not miss a church meeting. When he got home, Nob was completely exhausted. She could not eat or lie down. She gasped for breath and bled from the mouth. Finally, Nob lay down and died. All the family, except Daniel Muir, gathered around her, weeping.[6]

John never forgave his father for treating the farm animals harshly. In *The Story of My Boyhood and Youth*, the autobiography of his early years, Muir recounted these incidents and others. His sister Joanna cried as she read the first few chapters. "I wished with all my heart it had not been so true," she told her brother John.[7]

a neighboring town, the family made the most of his absence. The children joked and sang. The girls worked on their lace and embroidery. Their mother shared their fun, laughing as John, the family clown, recited a silly poem, danced a highland fling (a Scottish folk dance), or puffed out his cheeks and pretended to play the bagpipes.[8]

Another Farm, More Work

When John was seventeen, his father bought another farm, Hickory Hill, about six miles southeast of Fountain Lake, and the hard work began all over again. This time, John's job was to dig a well. Digging through the first ten feet was fairly easy. Then he hit a hard layer that had to be chipped away. Daniel, who never went down into the well himself, lowered John in a bucket to the bottom of the poorly ventilated shaft. He left his son chipping away until lunch. After eating, John was again lowered into the well. One morning, when the hole was about eighty feet deep, John began to feel faint even before he reached the bottom. By the time his father realized that something was wrong and hauled him up, John was unconscious. William Duncan, a neighbor who had been a miner, told the Muirs John was lucky to have survived the deadly choke-damp, a suffocating mixture of carbon monoxide and nitrogen gases. Duncan taught Daniel and John how to test for the heavy gas that could settle on the well-bottom overnight, and clear the air. Then John resumed chipping.

An Inventive Mind

Sometime during his teenage years, with the little spare time he had, John began to study mathematics. He persuaded his father to buy him an arithmetic book and was surprised to find that the elementary rules he had been forced to learn in Scotland actually made sense.[9] He worked out problems on chips of wood from chopped trees and mastered algebra, geometry, and trigonometry, one after the other.

The more John read, the more he wanted to learn. He treasured good literature and discovered that the poetry of the Bible, William Shakespeare, and John Milton were "sources of inspiring pleasure."[10] But John found little time to read, even on winter evenings when most chores were completed by sundown. His father expected everyone to go to bed immediately after family worship, which was often over by eight o'clock. One evening, as John tried to continue reading about church history after bedtime, his father called, "John, go to bed! Must I give you a separate order every night?" Then, as if realizing that his words were too harsh for an offense as forgivable as reading a religious book,

Daniel Muir added, "If you will read, get up in the morning . . . You may get up . . . as early as you like."[11]

The very next morning, John woke early, jumped out of bed, and rushed downstairs. The kitchen clock read one o'clock. John was overjoyed. "Five hours to myself, five huge, solid hours," he wrote later.[12] However, it was too cold to read. Knowing that his father would surely object if he built a fire, John decided to go down to the cellar and work on an invention he had been thinking about—a self-setting sawmill.

From then on, John got up every morning at "the same glorious hour" to work in the cellar, even though the temperature was freezing.[13] He completed the sawmill, then began other projects such as waterwheels, unusual door locks and latches, an automatic horse feeder, barometers, and thermometers. He also built his own clocks, even though he had never seen the inside of one. His first clock looked rather like a piece of farm machinery, but it kept time, and struck the hours. Daniel Muir was impressed and allowed the contraption to be set up in the parlor. John also made a clock-operated bed that he called "the early rising machine."[14] Their neighbor William Duncan often drove over in the evenings to bring John books and to admire his gadgets and inventions.

On a summer evening in 1860, Duncan brought John a newspaper. It described the Wisconsin State Agricultural Fair that was to be held in Madison in September. Duncan encouraged John to exhibit his inventions at the fair. He was sure that it would help the young inventor find work in a machine shop in the city.

Now twenty-two, John decided to take Duncan's advice. He told his father he planned to leave and asked if he could depend on getting some money from home, if he needed it. Daniel Muir said no: "Depend entirely on yourself."[15] So, with his grandfather's gold sovereign (a British coin), another gold piece from his mother, and a little money earned by growing wheat on an unused patch of ground, John Muir set out to start a new life on his own.

4

INVENTOR, STUDENT, AND BOTANIST

The Madison State Fair Grounds were bustling with activity in the fall of 1860 when John Muir arrived. It took the young, shaggy-bearded inventor only a few minutes to rig up his early-rising machine and attract a curious crowd. When one of the judges, Jeanne C. Carr, arrived at the booth, she discovered a long line of boys, including her own two sons, waiting impatiently to try out Muir's amazing contraption. One by one, the boys climbed into the improvised bed connected to a homemade clock. They would shut their eyes and pretend to be asleep. As the clock moved, the bed began to tilt up until it set each sleepyhead on his feet on the footboard.

Muir also displayed two clocks he had whittled from pinewood. One showed the hours, minutes, seconds, and the day of the month. The second was shaped like a scythe, a farm tool used to cut grain by hand. Its wooden wheels were arranged along the narrow blade. All the working parts were suspended inside a miniature burr oak tree with moss decorating its roots. A local newspaper reporter predicted "that few articles [would] attract as much attention as these products of Mr. Muir's ingenuity."[1]

Jeanne Carr was impressed by Muir's inventions and by his patience as the inventor cheerfully answered all the boys' questions while repeating the experiment over and over.[2] The young man was awarded a special cash prize of fifteen dollars on her recommendation. As his neighbor predicted, Muir's inventions had indeed opened the door to a new world.

The University

After working briefly for another inventor he met at the state fair, Muir applied for admission to the University of Wisconsin, and was accepted. Tuition for a twenty-week term was six dollars. In addition, Muir had to pay ten dollars for his room in North Hall. Those expenses consumed most of his money and he had to eat cheaply. His regular diet often consisted of graham crackers, potatoes, bread,

In 1861, John Muir invented his mechanical study desk to keep himself on task.

molasses, and water. He had no complaints, though. To him, the opportunity to learn was more important than food.

Jeanne Carr, the judge from the State Fair, and her husband, Dr. Ezra Carr, a professor of natural sciences at the university, followed Muir's progress with interest. Muir visited the family often and even helped look after their two boys. Jeanne Carr became a life-long friend and mentor for the young student. Muir enrolled in Dr. Carr's geology classes and studied how ice had shaped much of the earth's landscape. He selected other classes that he felt would be useful such as chemistry, physics, Greek, Latin, and botany.

A New Muir

By the time Muir went home to spend the summer with his family, he had learned some important

Civil War

In 1860, Abraham Lincoln was elected as the sixteenth president of the United States. While Muir studied in Wisconsin that winter and spring, many attempts were made to settle the differences between the free North and the slaveholding South. University students debated the issues: possible civil war, Lincoln's policies, slavery, and the right of Southern states to secede from the Union to form their own Confederacy.

Then, on April 12, 1861, Confederate troops fired on Fort Sumter in Charleston, South Carolina. Union soldiers inside the fort fired back, and the Civil War began. Many university students rushed to join the battle, but Muir seemed unaffected. He did not even mention the war in letters he wrote to his family.

things about himself. He knew his own worth and insisted that his father pay him seventy-five cents a day. Muir also realized that his hard work now served his own purpose. All the wages he earned plowing, chopping, hoeing, and harvesting would allow him to return to his studies in the fall.

At the end of August, Muir took his hard-earned dollars and returned to Madison. The town had changed. The state fairgrounds, only a half-mile west of the university, was now Camp Randall, a city of canvas tents filled with soldiers in training.

There were fewer students on campus. Many had dropped out to enlist in the Union army for three months.

Muir frequently visited Camp Randall recruits who were friends he had met at the university. When the Seventh Wisconsin Regiment left for the front, he went to the station to see them off. He could tell that many of the young soldiers were expecting a great patriotic adventure, but Muir recognized the realities of the battlefield. He knew that many of his friends would not return.

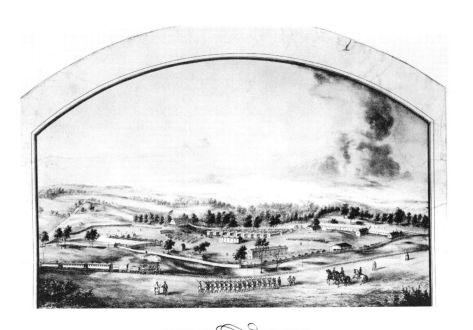

By the fall 1861, the state fairgrounds in Wisconsin had been transformed into Camp Randall. The hall where Muir exhibited his inventions is the most distant building on the left.

After that, he focused completely on his studies, and others were often amused by how hard he worked. The young man seemed to fear that he might be wasting precious time. To keep himself on task, Muir created a mechanical study desk. He described the way it worked: "Each morning the first book to be studied was pushed up from a rack below the top of the desk, thrown open, and allowed to remain there the number of minutes required. Then the machinery closed the book and allowed it to drop back into its stall, then move the rack forward and threw up the next in order, and so on."[3]

Muir was considered a campus character.[4] Visitors were often sent to look at his room, lined with shelves. These shelves were filled with glass tubes and jars, botanical and geological specimens, and small mechanical inventions. On the floor were other larger machines that left observers wondering what the gadgets might do.

The Study of Botany

During his second year, Muir became fascinated with botany and enrolled in classes taught by Dr. James Davie Butler. Hunting, collecting, and analyzing plants seemed like play to Muir and opened his eyes to the wonders of the natural world.

Only John Muir

John Muir was poor and appeared unsophisticated, but people liked his directness, his earnestness, and his cheerful energy. He would often do things that were considered odd. Once, when invited to a reception at the home of a professor, Muir became so intrigued with the workings of a piano that he actually climbed into the instrument for a closer inspection. A witness to this episode remarked that "it was all right with everyone there—since it was John Muir."[5]

From Professor Butler, Muir learned to observe plants carefully and to record even the tiniest of details. Butler also encouraged his students to keep a "commonplace book" or journal.[6] This became a habit for Muir. He always carried a small notebook to record his observations and thoughts.

After a second summer at home, twenty-five-year-old Muir headed back to the university. By now, the realities of war were everywhere. He saw the pain of the sick and wounded as they returned home. Muir understood how much they had sacrificed.

There were even rumors that the university itself would soon be forced to close after President

John Muir had his first photo taken in 1863 and sent a copy home, though he knew his father would disapprove. Daniel Muir's acceptance of the picture encouraged John's sisters and mother to have pictures taken.

Lincoln called for three hundred thousand volunteers to serve not for three months—but for three years. In the midst of all this, Muir said he loved his studies more than ever.[7] When he left the University of Wisconsin in June 1863, he had decided to study medicine the following year, an idea encouraged by the Carrs and Dr. Butler. They recognized Muir as a gifted student.

No one really knows why, but during the next few months, Muir's plans changed. Congress had passed the Enrollment Act in March 1863, making all male citizens twenty to forty-five years old eligible for military duty. Many immigrant families like the Muirs felt no strong allegiance to the United States and did not want to send their sons into battle. To avoid the draft, many young men decided to run away to Canada. Muir's youngest brother, Daniel, had already gone north. Finally, in March 1864, even though he had not been drafted, John Muir decided to go to Ontario, Canada, where his brother lived.

The Canadian Wilderness

The trip took several months. Muir tramped across the Canadian wilderness, collecting plants. He met few people along the way. He missed the friends and family he had left behind. However, Muir always remembered one incredible moment during this lonely journey. He had been wading for hours through a huge swamp, and was exhausted, cold, and discouraged. Then he discovered "the rarest and most beautiful of the flowering plants . . . a *Calypso borealis*, (the Hider of the North) . . . On a bed of yellow mosses . . . from which its one leaf and one flower [had] sprung. No other bloom was near it."[8] Its beauty was so unexpected and so surprising that

Muir sat down beside it and wept.[9] This beautiful flower gave Muir the inspiration for his first published writing, an essay called "the Calypso Borealis," which was published in the *Boston Recorder* in 1866.

By September 1864, John and Daniel were living together in Medford, Ontario. The two brothers worked in a factory that made rake, broom, and fork handles. John Muir was assigned the task of improving the efficiency of the lathe, a machine that turned square sticks into rounded broom handles. By inventing a self-feeding machine to take the place of the old hand-feed one, Muir succeeded in nearly doubling the number of brooms produced.

The following spring, the brothers learned that the Civil War was over. Confederate General Robert E. Lee had surrendered at Appomattox Court House, Virginia, on April 9, 1865. The South had lost. The Union was back together. Daniel Muir left for home immediately. John Muir stayed in Medford for another year, working in the factory and collecting botany samples.

Back to the United States

In 1866, about the time Muir turned twenty-eight, he decided to go back to the United States. After studying a map, he headed for Indianapolis, Indiana, a railroad town likely to have many machine shops and factories. The city was also surrounded by one of the richest hardwood forests on the continent. Like many towns in the North, Indianapolis had profited greatly from the war. Its factories had worked steadily to produce materials needed to support the Union war effort. When Muir arrived, the city was growing rapidly. To clear land for city lots and streets, forests had been cut down and wastefully burned.

Muir quickly found work at a factory that made carriage wheels, barrel staves, and plow handles. When he was hired, he told the company's owner that he only planned to stay long enough to earn the money needed for his dream trip to South America. However, Muir's talents were quickly recognized. The owners offered him a position as foreman, and even hinted about a possible partnership, so Muir stayed longer than he had planned. Soon he found less time to botanize as he spent long hours repairing and improving the factory's machines.

An Eye for Nature

Then on March 6, 1867, an on-the-job accident changed Muir's life. As he used a file to tighten a belt, the file slipped, flew up, and the nail-like end pierced his right eye. Muir covered his eye with his hand and when he pulled it away, his palm was covered with the aqueous humor, the liquid that fills the eye. The sight in his eye began to fade immediately and was soon gone. An assistant, who witnessed the accident, heard Muir whisper, "My right eye is gone, closed forever on all God's beauty."[10]

The shock sent him to bed. In his despair, Muir scribbled notes and sent them off to family and friends. When the Carrs and Dr. Butler learned of the accident, they sent a specialist to examine their friend. The specialist assured Muir that he would be able to see again, though the sight in his right eye would never be perfect. Then his left eye also failed—probably a sympathetic reaction caused by the shock. Muir was blind.

For the next month, Muir had to remain in a dark room while the vision in his left eye gradually returned. His right eye also got better. During this time the young man thought about what he wanted to do with his life. Muir decided to turn his eyes to the fields and woods. He quit his job with the carriage factory, and set off for Portage, Wisconsin, to complete his recovery among family and friends. Then he intended to go south into the wilderness and the tropics on a thousand-mile walk.

Later, he would write, "I might have become a millionaire, but I chose to become a tramp . . . walk through the woods, climb the hills and mountains, and live among the rocks and trees."[11]

5

ROAD TO
YOSEMITE

John Muir returned to Indianapolis near the end
of August, and on the first day of September
1867, he began his journey. He took a train to
Jeffersonville, Indiana then crossed the Ohio River
and walked south through Louisville, Kentucky.
When he reached the forest beyond the city, he
spread out his map and planned his route—the
"wildest, leafiest, and least trodden" one.[1] Muir
tramped south through Kentucky and explored
Mammoth Cave (The longest cave system in the
world, preserved today as a national park.) in
the central part of that state. By September 10, he
reached the summit of the Tennessee's Cumberland
Mountains—the first he had ever climbed.

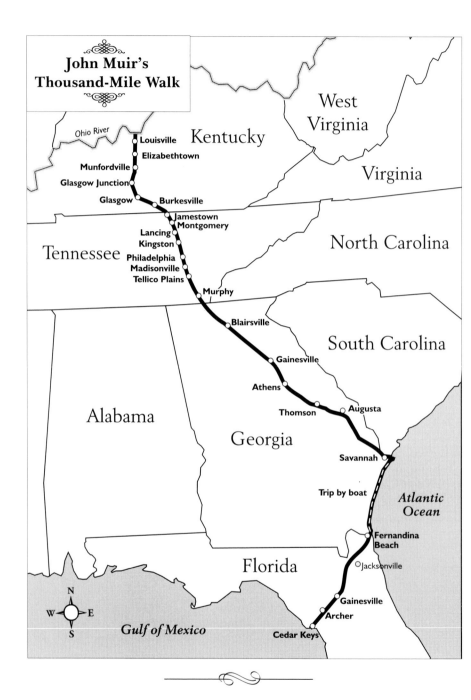

Ohio River
Louisville
Kentucky
West
Virginia
Elizabethtown
Munfordville
Virginia
Glasgow Junction
Glasgow
Burkesville
Jamestown
Montgomery
Lancing
Kingston
North Carolina
Tennessee
Philadelphia
Madisonville
Tellico Plains
Murphy
Blairsville
South Carolina
Gainesville
Athens
Augusta
Alabama
Thomson
Georgia
Savannah
Trip by boat
Atlantic
Ocean
Fernandina
Beach
Florida
Jacksonville
N
W   E
S
Gulf of Mexico
Gainesville
Archer
Cedar Keys

*John Muir took an amazing thousand-mile walk following the route
seen here.*

Along the way, Muir discovered an amazing variety of plants and trees and met some interesting people. One young man on horseback kindly offered to carry his heavy bag. Muir realized that the offer was really a thief's trick. The man wanted to steal his valuables. Muir did hand over his bundle. However, the thief was disappointed since any money Muir had brought along was not inside. What he found—a comb, map, plant press (a botanist's tool used to flattened and preserve plants), and a New Testament—were only important to Muir. After handing the bag back to its owner, the young man rode off.

People were often puzzled by the idea of a grown man walking a thousand miles just to look at plants. A blacksmith who gave Muir shelter one night expressed this opinion: ". . . surely you are able to do something better than wander over the country and look at weeds and blossoms. These are hard times, and real work is required of every man that is able."[2]

Unconcerned with others' opinions, Muir continued on his way. As he traveled deeper into the south, he saw more evidence of hard times. Most people were penniless and many farms were deserted because the owners had been killed or driven away during Civil War battles. Settlers were struggling to rebuild.

By early October, he had walked as far as
Savannah, Georgia. There, he expected to find mail
from home and money—his own, of course, that he
had asked his brother to send. However, no letters
or cash were waiting for him.

Since he had no way of knowing when the
money would arrive, Muir needed to save his last
dollar and a half for food. He decided to look for a
safe place to camp. After walking three or four miles
from the city, Muir discovered the Bonaventure
Cemetery. Feeling confident that no one would
bother him, he slept with his head resting on a grave.

The next morning, after eating a cracker or two
for breakfast, Muir returned to Savannah, but his
money had still not arrived. So, Muir went back to
the graveyard to make "a nest."[3] Using four bushes
as corner posts, he constructed a hut. He tied small
branches between the bushes, covered the top with
rushes, and spread moss to form a thick
mattress. Muir spent five or six days camped in the
graveyard, living on crackers and water. When
his money did arrive, the hungry man immediately
treated himself to a real meal and some fresh-baked
gingerbread.

Then, he booked passage on a steamship to
Florida on October 15, 1867. While tramping across
the peninsula, Muir contracted malaria, a disease
transmitted by infected mosquitoes. The family he

was boarding with nursed Muir for weeks while his body fought the high fever. After he recovered, Muir traveled to Cuba, but he was not well enough to explore the island's mountains or the wilds of South America. Instead, he set sail for San Francisco, California by a roundabout route. Muir first went by steamer to New York City. From there, he sailed to the Isthmus of Panama, hiked overland to the Pacific, and boarded another ship headed for Northern California.

Love at First Sight

Now almost thirty years old, Muir and a companion he'd met on the ship left the city as quickly as possible and headed for Yosemite Valley—a place Muir had read about while recovering from his eye injury. It was early April 1868 when they hiked through the San Joaquin Valley, "the Floweriest piece of the world I ever walked," Muir recorded.[4] The two men climbed up into the foothills where Muir viewed the Sierra Nevada mountains for the first time. Though they were still one hundred miles away, the sunlit, snowy peaks were awe-inspiring.

The hikers soon reached the rim of Yosemite Valley, where Muir caught his first glimpse of Bridal Veil Falls. "See that dainty little waterfall over there," he said. "It looks small from here, only about fifteen or twenty feet, but it may be sixty or

Half Dome towers over the end of Yosemite Valley. John Muir believed that a glacier had sliced off almost half of the mountain's granite dome.

seventy."[5] In reality, Bridal Veil Falls drops over six hundred twenty feet. For eight days, Muir camped in Yosemite. He sketched, explored the falls, collected plants, and studied the trees. He wanted to spend more time there, but first he needed money—for supplies and to help his younger sister. Mary had run away from home after their father had thrown her sketches into a mud puddle—to save her soul. With the money Muir sent, Mary entered the University of Wisconsin to study art, music, and botany.

Muir went to work a few miles from Yosemite for a rancher in the San Joaquin Valley taming wild horses, harvesting, and tending sheep. He preferred shepherding, since that job took him into the mountains. However, Muir soon realized that sheep picked their pastures bare, destroying the grasses and wildflowers. He nicknamed the woolly creatures "hoofed locusts."[6]

During his second summer in California, Muir was promoted to overseer of a large flock. The shepherd who worked under his supervision did most of the work. Muir now had more time to climb the peaks, hike the canyons, botanize, and study the rocks, soil, and water. He began to develop his own ideas about how geological forces had created the Sierra landscape.

One day, he noticed a smooth granite slab marked by deep, parallel scratches. Huge boulders, twenty to thirty feet in diameter, were scattered across the top of this slab. On close inspection, Muir discovered that the granite in the boulders was different from the granite of the slab they rested on. Remembering his studies of the Wisconsin Ice Age, Muir concluded that a glacier had brought the boulders here. When the river of ice melted, it left them behind. Gravel and sand on the bottom of the glacier had polished the smooth granite slab, and hard stones embedded in the ice had made the parallel scratches. The whole area, Muir realized, must have been covered by a thick sheet of ice. "A great discovery,"[7] he wrote in his journal.

Later that summer, Muir hiked to the edge of the cliff where Yosemite Falls tumbled over and "down half a mile in snowy foam,"[8] to the valley below. Hoping to observe the fall's descent more closely, Muir took off his shoes and stockings. He worked his way along the polished rock near the stream as the water roared past his head. When he reached the edge, a rocky shelf blocked his view. Then Muir spotted a narrow ledge about three inches wide on the very brink and looked for a way to get down to it. He finally saw a vertical crack in the rock that might offer some slight finger-holds. But the steeply pitched rock on either side of the crack was polished smooth. At first Muir decided not to try it. But the temptation to observe the waterfall was too great. With extreme caution he inched his way along the rough edge, until he could set his heels on the narrow ledge below. Then Muir shuffled along the ledge twenty or thirty feet so he could look directly "down into the . . . snowy . . ., comet-like streamers."[9]

Peering over the edge of the waterfall was thrilling. Later Muir had no idea how long he stood there, or how he got off the ledge, but he promised himself never to try anything that risky again.[10]

A Home in Yosemite Valley

In the fall of 1869, Muir was invited to visit his old friends, the Carrs, in Oakland. They had moved west that summer so the professor could teach at the University of California. Though he had not seen his friends for two years, Muir declined their invitation. With the money he had saved from his sheep-tending job, he could now go back to Yosemite.

By November, Muir had found a job in Yosemite Valley working for hotel owner James M. Hutchings. Hutchings, the valley's first permanent resident, had advertised this beautiful region in his *Illustrated California Magazine*, published from 1856 to 1861.

Hutchings hired Muir to build and operate a sawmill. It would be used to cut up trees that had been blown over during storms. As part of the agreement, Muir was free to explore when he was not needed at the sawmill.

Muir built himself a cabin on the banks of Yosemite Creek near the mill with materials that cost three dollars. Part of the stream flowed through one corner of the room, so he could enjoy the sound of running water, inside or out. The floor was made of rough wood boards laid on the ground. Ferns grew up between the cracks. Muir trained some of these plants to grow up strings he tied along the sides and top of a window. The ferns formed a leafy green arch under which he placed his writing desk. His bed hung from the rafters.

Tour Guide

When Muir, now thirty-three, was not needed to run the sawmill, Hutchings sometimes asked him to guide tourists about the valley. Muir disliked this duty because it interfered with his time to explore and study geological features, but there was one notable exception.

In April 1871, Ralph Waldo Emerson, the famous writer and philosopher, arrived. Muir who was familiar with Emerson's work, gladly showed the sixty-eight-year-old gentleman Yosemite's natural wonders.[11] He invited Emerson into his home to see his collection of plants and sketches. Muir also proposed a camping trip into the mountains, but members of Emerson's party insisted that he stay at the hotel and on the valley trails. When Muir escorted the group to Mariposa Big Tree Grove, again he hoped to camp, but again he was disappointed. When the group left the grove to return to civilization, Emerson was the last to reach the ridge top. There he turned his horse, took off his hat, and waved a last good-bye to his new friend.

Muir went back to the grove to camp. For the first time in these forests, he felt lonesome. Then he "took heart again—the trees had not gone to Boston,

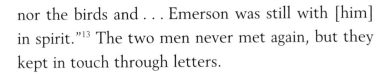

Abraham Lincoln and Yosemite

In 1864, President Abraham Lincoln signed a bill that granted Yosemite Valley, "the 'Cleft' or 'Gorge' in the granite peak of the Sierra Nevada, to the State of California." The act declared that "the premises shall be held for public use, resort, and recreation."[12] The Mariposa Big Tree Grove, a stand of sequoias, some of the largest trees on earth, was also included in the grant.

By the time John Muir made his home in the valley, about one thousand tourists visited the area each year.

nor the birds and . . . Emerson was still with [him] in spirit."[13] The two men never met again, but they kept in touch through letters.

Glacier Studies

At thirty-four, John Muir had shaggy, reddish-brown hair and a full beard. He was suntanned, lean, and muscular. As he tramped into the backcountry, the explorer wore baggy trousers, a wool shirt, a vest with pockets to carry small items, and a brimmed hat. He wore heavy-soled shoes that came up above his ankles. He carried a light ax, a watch, a pocket lens, a thermometer, a compass, a knife, and spectacles to protect his eyes from the sun's glare. Muir worried little about what he ate and carried only bread and tea.

In the summer of 1871, Muir climbed to a canyon beside Yosemite Falls. Up the canyon he discovered a narrow gorge with walls polished and deeply grooved–proof that a glacier had wedged through under great pressure. The canyon's sides were lined with rocks, gravel, and sand. This debris, called a lateral moraine, is carried along by the edge of the glacier and left behind when the ice melts. He followed the glacier's trail to a shallow hollow in the side of eleven-thousand-foot Mount Hoffman (a peak in the Sierra Nevada range near the center of

Earthquake

Muir experienced his first earthquake while living in Yosemite Valley. When the "wild thrilling motion and rumbling" began about two o'clock in the morning, Muir ran out of his cabin and shouted, "A Noble earthquake." [14] He took shelter behind a big pine afraid that the three-thousand-foot cliff called Sentinel Rock would come crashing down. Then he heard a tremendous roar a short distance up the valley. Eagle Rock, a formation high on the valley's south wall, had given way. The quake was over in a few minutes, and Muir ran up the moonlit valley and climbed the fallen boulders before they were completely at rest.

Yosemite National Park). This discovery assured Muir that ice had flowed into Yosemite Valley carving the walls and slicing off Half Dome.

In September, after summarizing his conclusions in an article that he sent to the *New York Tribune,* Muir continued his research near Mount Merced on the eastern edge of the mountain range. He followed a stream that was bordered by ice and bare earth. No plants grew nearby. The water in the stream was gray. Muir dipped his hand in. When he pulled it out, his fingers were covered with a gritty paste. "Glacier mud!"[15] he said to himself. John Muir had found his first living glacier in the Sierras—a flowing glacier that was being replenished from the ice field where it began.

6

SCIENTIST, AUTHOR, AND EXPLORER

Muir's theory—that Yosemite Valley had been filled from wall to wall with a glacier some three thousand feet thick—contradicted the beliefs of most noted geologists of his day. In fact, Josiah D. Whitney, the chief geologist of California, had determined that glaciers had played an insignificant role in the carving of Yosemite and the landscape of the Sierra Nevada Mountains. He believed that Yosemite had been created when the bottom of the valley sank after a severe earthquake. Muir respected Whitney, but believed he was wrong about Sierra glaciers, and said so.

When Whitney learned that Muir was claiming Yosemite had been carved by glaciers, the professor dismissed his theory with one sentence: "What does that sheepherder know about it?"[1]

Muir continued his research and found glaciers on Mount Lyell and Mount McClure, peaks on the eastern edge of the Sierra Nevadas. This time, the self-taught scientist pounded a line of stakes into the McClure Glacier—an experiment to measure the movement of the ice. When he returned to check the line forty-five days later, Muir discovered that the middle stakes had moved about forty-five inches—or at the rate of an inch a day. This glacier was alive and was still at work, shaping the mountain landscape. Muir eventually located sixty-five glaciers in the Sierras.

Author

For some time, Jeanne Carr had encouraged Muir to publish his glacier research—before others took credit for it. Finally, in 1873, Muir decided to take her advice and try to earn a living by writing.

So after a solo ascent of Mount Whitney, California's highest peak, Muir went to Oakland in November. There, he began writing a series of articles on Sierra glaciers and mountain sculpture for the *Overland Monthly*. For the next ten months, Muir labored away with his pen. It did not take him long to realize that writing was hard, tedious, and lonely work.[2] When he needed a break, he spent time with his friends, the Carrs. That spring, Jeanne Carr introduced Muir to Dr. John Theophile Strentzel, his wife, Louisiana, and their twenty-seven-year-old daughter, Louie (short for Louisiana). The family invited Muir to visit their ranch outside the city, but when his work was done in September 1874, Muir hurried back to his mountains.

Muir's six articles of the "Studies in the Sierra" series were published in the *Overland Monthly*, a Pacific Coast literary journal between May 1874 and January 1875. Though these articles would eventually be recognized as an important scientific contribution, they did not immediately earn Muir respect as a scientist. One reason for this was that the *Overland Monthly* was a popular, general publication, not a scientific journal. However, the strongest negative factor was Whitney's strong influence in the geological community.

New Horizons

On his return to Yosemite, Muir wrote that "none of the rocks [in Yosemite] seem to call me now."[3] It was time to explore new territory. He decided to go to central Oregon and study Mount Shasta's glaciers. He set off along the main stagecoach route between California and Oregon in late October. When he arrived, he discovered that no one was willing to climb the mountain with winter approaching. So he went alone. When he reached an elevation of nine thousand feet, Muir realized a storm was coming. He made camp, collected plenty of firewood, and prepared to enjoy the Shasta storm. For several days, Muir recorded his observations—the way snow collected on the trees, how a squirrel found nuts hidden under the drifts, and the behavior of wild sheep. Muir was disappointed when a guide from the hotel at the base of the mountain rode up and "rescued" him on the fifth day of the storm.[4]

On a second trip to Shasta, Muir again got caught by a storm. As he struggled to get down off the glacier, Muir's feet froze. For the rest of his life cold temperatures made his feet ache, but that did not prevent him from climbing more mountains in all kinds of weather.

At age thirty-seven, Muir found he could no longer be a man of the wilderness all the time. Now he spent his summers traveling and his winters writing articles. His writing provided money for his few needs, but more importantly, allowed Muir to save a little money. He continued to send funds home to help his younger brother Daniel and Mary with college and take care of their mother. Ann had chosen to stay in Portage when her husband Daniel sold his farms and went to Canada to join a church group.

John Muir camped in a snowstorm on Oregon's Mount Shasta and was disappointed when a guide from the hotel at the base of the mountain rode up and "rescued" him.

In January 1876, Muir gave his first public lecture on glaciers and forests in Sacramento, California. He was extremely nervous about making the speech[5] so artist and friend William Keith gave Muir a mountain landscape to take on stage with him. Keith told Muir that if he looked at the painting, he would forget his nervousness. This strange idea helped Muir overcome his fear and the speech was a great success.

That same month, Muir also wrote his first essay on forest conservation. Called "God's First Temples:

How Shall We Preserve Our Forests?" it was published in the *Sacramento Record-Union*. In this tough, uncompromising essay, Muir claimed that the destruction of the Sierra forests was proceeding so rapidly that the slopes would soon be stripped and the lowlands flooded by waters that had been stored by the forest's root systems. Once destroyed, Muir knew these natural treasures could not be replaced, even with centuries of careful replanting. Muir recommended passing laws to prevent this disaster—not a popular solution at that time.

A New Love

As he returned from his travels during the summer of 1877, Muir decided to accept the Strentzels'

A Wild Tree Ride

John Muir was always looking for new ways to get close to nature. During a violent windstorm in December 1874, Muir decided to climb a tree to be close "to the music of its topmost needles."[6] Clinging to his treetop seat in the tall Douglas fir, Muir estimated its wildest sweep made an arc of some twenty to thirty degrees. He thoroughly enjoyed his view of the wind-blown forest and climbed down only when the storm was over several hours later.[7]

three-year-old invitation to visit their ranch near Martinez, California. Before long, it was clear that Muir was attracted to their thirty-year-old daughter.[8] Louie, a pleasant-looking woman with high cheekbones and gray eyes, was well-educated and an accomplished pianist. She lived with her parents and helped her father with his fruit business.

That winter and spring, Muir often set aside his writing to visit the Strentzels. The bearded, casually dressed man and the quiet, well-dressed woman often walked the hills and orchards surrounding her home. Though he kept detailed journals about almost everything else, Muir recorded little information about their relationship. While traveling, he wrote letters, obviously intended for Louie, but addressed them to Dr. and Mrs. Strentzel.

In June 1879, Muir asked Louie to marry him. She accepted. However, the two agreed not to announce their engagement until Muir returned from one more adventure. This time, he planned to go north to Alaska. He did not know how long he would be gone.

Explorer

In July 1879, when Muir arrived by ship at Fort Wrangell located on an island (Wrangell Island) in the Alaskan panhandle, the territory had been part of the United States for a little over a decade.

Presbyterian missionary S. Hall Young was among the group waiting for the ship that arrived once a month with mail and supplies. Surrounded by new, unexplored territory, Muir began his studies as soon as he got ashore. Young and others who lived at the fort quickly learned that it was not unusual to find Muir tramping in the damp woods or crawling about on the forest floor to examine the plant life—day or night.

One stormy night, the village natives were alarmed by a strange glow on the hill behind the village. They feared that evil spirits were at work and asked Young to protect them. No spirits were afoot—only John Muir. He had climbed the hill during the storm and built himself a huge bonfire so he could observe how "these Alaskan trees behaved in wind and rain, and hear the songs they sang."[9] Young appreciated Muir's curiosity about the environment and began to accompany him on botanical hikes.

For Muir, the highlight of his first Alaskan trip was a canoe voyage of almost eight hundred miles into Glacier Bay. He is believed to be the first white man to explore that watery region. Since the group planned to stop along the way at tribal villages, Young agreed to go along. He helped Muir find a crew. They left Fort Wrangell on October 14, 1879. The sun was shining, a rare event for that time of the year, but the native crew was not cheerful.

Winter was coming. Snow would fall soon. They expected that their canoe would be crushed by ice as the waterways Muir intended to explore froze.[10]

Ten days later, the party camped near the mouth of Glacier Bay. The very next morning, they paddled into unexplored waters. By noon, the canoe passed the first of the bay's glaciers. Muir could barely see its blue cliffs through the heavy rain, but he clearly heard the roar of falling icebergs.

Muir wanted to keep traveling up the bay to other, bigger ice mountains. But their guide insisted

An Amazing Rescue

On one hike to a mountain summit, the thirty-two-year-old S. Hall Young tried to keep up with Muir who was forty-three. In his haste, Young slipped and fell, dislocating both shoulders. With his feet hanging over the brink of a cliff, Young screamed for help. Muir climbed down to the injured man, took Young's collar in his teeth, and somehow got both of them back up to the spot where Young had slipped. Years later, Young still could not imagine how Muir had accomplished this incredible feat. Once on the ledge, Muir succeeded in setting one of Young's shoulders. Now Muir faced the task of getting his injured friend down the mountain in the dark. At times, Muir half carried the semi-conscious man. They reached help about seven-thirty the next morning.

that the glaciers at the head of the bay were too dangerous to approach except in full daylight. So, while the crew made camp, Muir explored the area. He soon realized that the landscape of this strange bay was still being born. It was a young Yosemite Valley being carved and polished by its rivers of ice.

The next morning, though it was snowing and raining off and on, Muir and his crew paddled on. They passed inlet after inlet, until they came to the last one and sailed up it about five miles. At the end, they discovered an ice wall two miles wide with

For John Muir, the highlight of his first Alaskan trip was a voyage of almost eight hundred miles made in twenty-five-foot canoes similar to the ones pictured here.

John Muir hoped to site a spectacular flowing glacier and snow-capped peak around every bend of Glacier Bay. Muir would have appreciated the view today from Glacier Bay's Jaw Bend.

icebergs clustered at its base. Muir wanted to get a better view and started up a nearby mountain. He had only climbed about one thousand feet when the clouds began to lift and streams of sunlight made the glacier and icebergs sparkle. Muir climbed higher. Soon he was looking out over a sea of ice, all the way to where these glaciers were born among the mountain peaks that formed Alaska's Fairweather Range (a range north and east of Glacier Bay). Muir thought nothing could be more majestic. The next morning, the crew was able to land near the glacier and Muir climbed its front by cutting steps between ice and rock.

As they paddled back to the main bay, ice was beginning to form between the icebergs. In some places, they had to break a lane for the canoe with the tent poles. Each day, the danger of being trapped by ice grew. Finally the ice was forming a barrier that the canoe could not be forced through. The crew was relieved when Muir finally had to give up climbing each mountain he could reach and exploring every inlet. They arrived at Fort Wrangell near the end of November, 1879. Among the mail waiting for Muir was a letter from Louie saying she wished that he could be home for Thanksgiving.[11] It was too late for that. The November mail boat had already gone. Muir would have to wait a month for the next one.

Mrs. Louie Strentzel Muir, wife of John Muir

7

FAMILY TIES

Whenen Muir and Louie were finally together again in February 1880, the couple announced their engagement and set their wedding date. Relatives and friends were completely surprised.[1] Most thought Muir would remain a bachelor. The groom-to-be was suddenly the center of attention, and that made him uncomfortable. He would have preferred to hide away in the nearest canyon.[2] However, one week before his forty-second birthday, on April 14, 1880, John Muir married thirty-three-year-old Louie Wanda Strentzel. To the groom's delight, rain poured from the clouds as the couple exchanged vows under apple blossom sprays that decorated the Strentzel home.[3]

As a wedding present, the bride's parents, who had built a new home for themselves, gave the newlyweds the family ranch house and twenty acres of orchards. The house sat on a hill surrounded by fruit trees. Ivy and roses cascaded from its wide verandas. It was a charming place for the couple to honeymoon.

Muir spent the next few months learning to care for the orchards and working in the fields. However, when the early crop was harvested, he made plans for another trip north.

Alaska Again

On July 30, 1880, Muir sailed again for Alaska. S. Hall Young was standing on the Fort Wrangell dock waiting for the mail boat when he spotted his friend John Muir. After a brief exchange of greetings, Muir immediately asked how soon Young could be ready to set sail to explore the ice-filled fiords. He planned to continue his studies of how glaciers, rivers of ice, changed the shape of the Alaskan landscape.

When Young suggested there was no hurry and asked why the explorer had not brought his wife with him, Muir exclaimed, "My wife could not come, so I have come alone and you've got to go with me to find the lost. Get your canoe and crew and let us be off."[4] That something Muir had lost, according to Young, was a glacier he had missed the year before.

During the eight days it took to prepare for the voyage, Muir wrote to Louie several times. Once the explorers sailed north from Fort Wrangell, there would be no way to send mail to her. Though Louie had probably agreed to her husband's second trip to Alaska even before they were married, some of her early letters show that she missed Muir when he traveled.[5]

With Young's help, Muir hired a crew of three, purchased provisions, and loaded everything into a twenty-five-foot canoe. As they were about to depart, Young's little dog, Stickeen, jumped aboard. Muir suggested that the "helpless creature"[6] would be in the way. However, the dog did not wish to be left behind. He curled up in a hollow among the baggage and held his ground. Stickeen had been named for the Indian guides' tribe, and they considered him good luck, so the dog was welcome.

Soon Muir and his companions were paddling north. They hoped to find a glacier-rimmed bay that the Indians called Sum Dum, later called Holokham Bay. There were no maps to guide the explorers, but this challenge did not discourage Muir. He had come for "ice work," as he called his glacier studies, and Sum Dum Bay promised him an abundance of spectacular icebergs.

Muir pushed his crew relentlessly. He had promised his wife that he would be home by the end of October, but he was also determined to discover all the glaciers he had missed the year before. They often paddled long after dark no matter what the weather.

Late one evening, the party reached Sum Dum Bay. In the morning, they watched as a large group of icebergs spilled from the bay's mouth, riding the outgoing tide. When the tide came in, Muir and his crew put their canoe into the water and paddled furiously to stay in front of the icebergs that were being carried back into the bay. They were forced to stop when they reached the bay's longest arm, the Endicott. Its narrow mouth was jammed with ice. After fitting the bow and stern of the boat with guards—long poles to keep the bergs at a safe distance—the crew worked their way through the floating ice. They shoved small icebergs aside and went around the giant ones until they again reached open water. The explorers traveled up the bay for fourteen hours, searching for Muir's lost glacier. The trip took so long that the crew began to tease Muir, saying that the Sum Dum Glacier did not care to show his face to the Ice Chief, their nickname for Muir.

Finally, they found a stream of ice three quarters of a mile wide and eight or nine hundred feet high.

The Mendenhall Glacier flows out of the Juneau ice fields, an area that John Muir explored. This glacier is more than a mile wide. The dark stripe in the middle, called a medial moraine, is rock debris that collected when two glaciers flowed together.

As Muir stood up in the canoe to sketch the glacier, several chunks broke loose and dropped into the water. "Your lost friend . . . is firing his guns in your honor," one member of the crew told Muir.[7] When he had completed his sketch, the "Ice Chief" noticed another canyon to the west. It was the home of a second glacier. As the first white man to explore this bay, Muir named the first glacier, Young, after his friend. Unfortunately, a chart-maker later renamed it. Today, it is known as Dawes Glacier.

On August 29, the party made camp near a great glacier in Taylor Bay west of the mouth of Glacier Bay. Muir soon noticed that this glacier was different. It was not receding, or shrinking, like the others he had observed. The ground in front of the icy mass was being lifted up and pushed toward the sea—an example of tremendous glacial power.

The next morning, Muir felt a "wild storm was blowing and calling"[8] and before anyone else was awake, he went off to explore. His only companion was Young's little dog, Stickeen. Muir later wrote about his adventure with a dog and a glacier. It was eventually published as a book, entitled *Stickeen*.

A Glacier Named Muir

When they left the campsite at Taylor Bay, the explorers sailed on into Glacier Bay. Muir spent an entire week trekking across the surface of a glacier that would later be named for him—with Stickeen at his heels. He always carried several handkerchiefs, but returned from one outing with none to spare. Muir had used them all to make moccasins for Stickeen, whose feet were cut and bleeding from the sharp ice of the glacial surface.

Another day, he and Young drove a straight line of stakes into the glacier. By watching the way the line changed, they learned that parts of this ice current flowed fifty or sixty feet a day.

The group spent another week exploring inlets and glaciers to the west, even though the weather was rainy and cold, and fog reduced visibility. Then, afraid that Muir would miss the monthly mail ship, his transportation back to California, they traveled two days and two nights without stopping.[9] They arrived in Sitka, the settlement closest to Glacier Bay on Baranof Island, in time. Muir found a letter

Travels in Alaska

To John Muir, Alaska was the one place on earth that equaled Yosemite Valley's grandeur. In total, he made seven trips to study the territory's unfamiliar plants, animals, and landscapes. He explored the arctic land on foot, by canoe, and by dogsled. At age fifty-two, the explorer loaded everything he needed on a sled about three feet long and spent ten days exploring Muir Glacier in Glacier Bay, alone. Near the end of his trip, he grew careless and stepped into a water-filled crevasse. The struggle to pull himself out took all his energy. He had to strip off his wet clothing, crawl into his sleeping bag, and spend the night trying to warm up.

On another trip, Muir paddled his canoe into a passage between two icebergs. When he was part way through, he suddenly discovered that his route was growing narrower. He backed out just as the ice walls came together with a crunch. John Muir wrote about these adventures and others in his last book, *Travels in Alaska*.

waiting for him from Louie. It had been written only a few weeks after he left home. She was very ill. (Her new husband was relieved when he finally reached home to find his wife not only well but pregnant.)[10]

They also found Captain L. A. Beardslee, the senior United States naval officer in Alaska waiting for them. He was extremely interested in their exploration. At his request, Muir and Young drew a rough map of Glacier Bay. The captain sent this map to the Navy Department with his annual report. He penciled the name Glacier Bay on the map. Beardslee also gave Muir's name to the glacier he had explored for a week, the bay's principal glacier.

Then it was time for Stickeen and Young to go back to their village home. The parting was sad. Muir carefully explained the matter to the little dog, Young wrote, "talking to and reasoning with him as if he were human," but as they paddled away Stickeen stood "on the stern of the canoe, howling a sad farewell."[11]

Young, too, never forgot "those great days . . . spent together. Nearly all of them were cold, wet and uncomfortable. . . . But these so-called 'hardships' Muir made nothing [of], and I caught his spirit; therefore the beauty, the glory, the wonder, and the thrill of those weeks of exploration are with me yet and shall endure—a [bountiful] treasure."

Family

Muir's daughter, Annie "Wanda," was born on March 25, 1881. Now almost forty-three, Muir was a father for the first time. In a letter to one of his sisters, he wrote "our own little big girl makes the home and the farm and the vineyard, and the hills, and the whole landscape far or near, shine for us."[12] Though he no longer was as free as a mountain breeze, Muir seemed pleased with his new life.

Having a daughter seemed to remind Muir that he had not seen his own parents, brothers, and sisters since he had left Wisconsin in 1867. He had a strong desire to visit his childhood home.[13] His trip home was also prompted by a sudden premonition that his father was dying. One morning in the fall of 1885, he suddenly laid down his pen and told Louie: "I am going East, because somehow I feel this morning that if I don't go now I won't see father again."[14] His father was living with Joanna, the youngest daughter in Kansas City, Kansas, but Muir first went to Portage to see his brother David, sisters Annie and Sarah, and his mother. Ann Muir was not well enough to travel, but John talked his brother and two sisters into going with him to Kansas City. They stopped in Lincoln, Nebraska, for brother Daniel, and sent for Margaret and Mary, who also lived in Nebraska. For the first time in more than twenty years, all the Muir children were with their father.

Daniel was confined to bed and spent his time reading the Bible. The brothers and sisters were with Daniel for three or four days before he died.

Back at the Ranch

For the first eight years of his married life, Muir worked hard to turn the ranch into a money-making business. He planted the vines and young trees himself. He converted hayfields into vineyards and orchards. He grew Bartlett pears, grapes, and cherries. Muir was a tough businessman. He studied the markets. He knew what his crops were worth and always drove a hard bargain. During this time, Muir also continued his studies. Each spring he escaped into the wilderness for several weeks. In 1884, he also took time to share the magnificent Yosemite Valley with Louie.

On January 23, 1886, the Muirs' second daughter, Helen, was born. The infant suffered from respiratory problems. During her first year and a half, Muir seldom left the ranch.

John Muir was a devoted father. As Wanda and Helen grew up, he took them on walks. He taught them the scientific names for plants and to love the wilderness just as he did. He often told them adventure stories of Paddy Grogan and his kangaroo steed, children's stories of his own creation.[15]

Unfortunately, these tales are lost forever. Muir never wrote them down.

Though Muir was quite successful as a rancher, Louie realized that the ranch work was responsible for her husband's illnesses. Frequently, he grew thin and developed a cough. Whenever her husband became ill, Louie would send him off to the wilderness—to regain his energy and to pursue his real work of studying nature. It was during these trips that Muir became concerned with the destruction being caused by lumbering and grazing. Most people at that time believed the country's natural resources would last forever. There was little support for the concept of laws to protect the wilderness.

Running the ranch had also interfered with Muir's writing. Louie and many of their friends wanted him to get back to his pen work, to use his writing talent to promote forest conservation. So in 1887, he agreed to edit and contribute to an illustrated book called *Picturesque California*. It was difficult for Muir to supervise his workmen on the ranch while trying to compose articles for the book. The job also required Muir to make several trips. He was not well when he left home on one of these trips. In a letter home, he expressed confidence that he would "be well at Shasta beneath a pine tree."[16] The excursion took him to Oregon's Mount Hood,

John Muir (far right) taught his daughters to love nature. Helen and Wanda (on horseback) often accompanied him on outings such as this one to Sequoia National Park. They are pictured in front of a giant sequoia, a tree that Muir worked to protect.

and Mount Rainer, the Columbia River, and Puget Sound in Washington State.

By 1888, Muir's efforts to turn the ranch into a profitable business were successful. The family was financially set. Louie encouraged John to hire some-one to manage the ranch, to concentrate on his books, and on the greatest work of his life—his defense of the wild places that he loved so well.

Today, California's Yosemite National Park has about 1,100 kilometers (700 miles) of trails. Visitors can see many of the sites that John Muir was marveled by.

8

CRUSADING FOR THE WILDERNESS

John Muir accompanied Robert Underwood Johnson, the editor of *Century Magazine*, to Yosemite Valley and the surrounding area in 1889. As they sat around a campfire in Tuolumne Meadows, Johnson suggested that the two of them work together on a special project—to see that the area neighboring the Yosemite Valley California State Park was preserved as a national park. Muir agreed to map the proposed boundaries for such a park and to write a series of articles to attract public support. Johnson agreed to present a proposal to the United States House of Representatives' Committee on Public Lands.

In August and September 1890, Muir's two articles, "The Treasures of Yosemite" and "Features of the Proposed Yosemite National Park," appeared in *Century Magazine*. His vivid style and his passion for the project attracted wide public support for the proposal Johnson introduced to Congress. The plan was successful. On October 1, 1890, the area earmarked by Muir became Yosemite National Park. Though it was not the first official national park, Yosemite helped establish the national park concept. (Yellowstone became the first national park in 1872.)

Pleased with these results, Muir immediately put his pen back to work on another article for *Century Magazine*.[1] This time, the author suggested that more big tree groves and the King's River region, located south of Yosemite in the Sierra Nevadas, be added to Sequoia National Park. Congress again responded positively by voting to enlarge Sequoia National Park and created General Grant National Park, known today as Kings Canyon.

The Sierra Club

By the 1890s, many Americans were beginning to see the need to protect their natural resources. Muir had been promoting conservation of trees and wild places since 1876, when his first essay on forest conservation was published. People across the country naturally looked to him for leadership. Muir supported new laws to protect the forests and to create additional reserves.

Knowing there would be strong resistance to many of Muir's ideas, friends encouraged him to find others who would support his efforts. On July 4, 1892, at the age of fifty-four, Muir helped establish the Sierra Club. The club had two primary goals: "to explore, enjoy, and [make] accessible the mountain regions of the Pacific Coast, [and] to publish authentic information concerning them." The second goal was "to enlist the support and cooperation of the people and government in preserving the forests and other natural features of the Sierra Nevada Mountains."[2] Membership included people who loved mountains and mountaineering as well as those who wanted to save the forests and other natural features for their children and grandchildren. Muir believed strongly in both of the club's goals and the twenty-seven founding members elected him the Sierra Club's first president, the position he would hold until his death.

Back to his Boyhood Days

The following year, Muir traveled east. He stopped in Wisconsin to visit his mother, spent a few days at the Chicago World's Fair, an exhibition that included displays from many nations. Near Boston,

Massachusetts, he toured the homes and graves of his friend Emerson and Henry David Thoreau. Both were transcendentalist authors and leaders of a movement that believed, as did Muir, an awareness of the beauty and truth of the surrounding natural world helped individuals reach their potential. Then Muir sailed across the Atlantic to his birthplace in Dunbar, Scotland.

When he returned home to California after more than four months of travel, Muir devoted most of his time to writing. His first book, *The Mountains of California*, was published in 1894. It emphasized Muir's belief that America's forests must be saved as national parks and reserves. The book received excellent reviews and the first edition sold quickly. The next year, Muir began a second book. This time the subject was Yosemite. He went back to the headwaters of the Tuolumne and to the Hetch Hetchy Valley to do research. As in the old days, he carried no blanket and few provisions. When the trip was over, the fifty-seven-year-old man wrote to his mother that,

> the six weeks of mountaineering . . . in my old haunts are over . . . But how I enjoyed this excursion . . . I suppose old age will put an end to scrambling in rocks and ice, but I can still climb as well as ever. I am trying to write another book, but that is harder than mountaineering.[3]

In June 1896, Muir was "suddenly possessed with the idea that [he] ought to go back to Portage, Wisconsin to see [his] mother once more."[4] Ann Muir died at the age of eighty-three, shortly after her son's visit.

Service to the Trees

For the next decade, Muir worked hard for conservation. In 1896, he was invited to serve on the first United States Forestry Commission, a committee that received no pay. The commission traveled through several western states to survey how existing public-owned lands were being used. Members were dismayed by the widespread damage they observed. Overgrazing near Oregon's Crater Lake had caused serious destruction of plant life. Lumber companies in California had illegally cut valuable forests. Trees surrounding Arizona's Grand Canyon were being cut, and mines were being dug in the canyon. When the commission reported their findings to President Grover Cleveland, he proclaimed thirteen forest reservations, now called national forests, protecting 25 million acres.

During these years, Muir continued to write. His articles, published in *Harper's Weekly* and *Atlantic Monthly*, created wide public support for forest preservation. At age sixty-three his book *Our National Parks* was published.

An Uneventful Life?

Many of Muir's friends encouraged him to write his autobiography. He thanked them for the suggestion, but stated that his "life on the whole has been level and uneventful, and therefore hard to make a book that many would read. I am not anxious to tell what I have done but what Nature has done—an infinitely more important story."[5]

President Theodore Roosevelt

In the spring of 1903, President Theodore Roosevelt spent several days touring California. Friends asked Muir to postpone a trip to Asia in order to accompany Roosevelt to Yosemite. Muir agreed.

Muir met the president at the Mariposa Big Trees Grove on May 15, 1903, and the two rode off for three days together in Yosemite. This was the beginning of a life-long friendship between the two men. Unfortunately, Muir's accounts of what happened during this time have been lost. Only a brief passage in a letter to his wife remains: "I had a perfectly glorious time with the President and the mountains. I never before had a more interesting, hearty, and manly companion."[6]

Roosevelt, already a friend of the forests, left Yosemite convinced that action must be taken to protect the nation's wild places. By the time he left office in 1909, Roosevelt had set aside more than 148 million acres of additional national forests and doubled the number of national parks. With the help of a special act that Congress passed during his

President Theodore Roosevelt and John Muir stand three thousand feet above Yosemite Valley on Glacier Point. Upper Yosemite Falls is visible in the background.

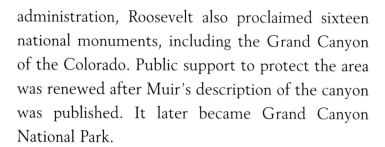

World Traveler
During this decade, Muir also found time to travel. He retraced parts of his thousand-mile trek to Florida and joined an expedition of scientists to explore the coast of Alaska. In 1903, he began a year-long tour to study the plants, trees, and geological features of England, France, Germany, Russia, Finland, Korea, Japan, China, India, Egypt, Ceylon, Australia, New Zealand, Malaya, Indonesia, the Philippines, Hong Kong, and Hawaii.

administration, Roosevelt also proclaimed sixteen national monuments, including the Grand Canyon of the Colorado. Public support to protect the area was renewed after Muir's description of the canyon was published. It later became Grand Canyon National Park.

Saving Yosemite Valley

Yosemite Valley had been a California state park since 1864 when Abraham Lincoln signed a bill giving the property held by the federal government to the state. After the creation of Yosemite National Park in 1890, Muir became concerned about the state's management of the valley. He believed the area would be better protected if it were part of the national park that surrounded it. Since one of the Sierra Club's goals was to protect the mountains, Muir hoped that club members would support his desire to give the valley back to the federal government. However, the club itself was made up primarily of Californians, and many members loyally supported state control.

Muir believed that "if every citizen could take one walk through [Yosemite Valley], there would be no more trouble about its care."[7] So he pursued another club goal—to explore the mountain regions—as a way to win public support for his idea. He supported and participated in outings planned by the Sierra Club. These organized adventures to view some of the grandest scenery of the Sierras sparked public interest in the mountains and also promoted the idea that a national park should encourage those unfamiliar with the out-of-doors to explore and enjoy the wilderness.

By January 1905, Muir finally convinced club members that the return of Yosemite Valley to the federal government was essential. With his help, the Sierra Club prepared a statement listing the reasons its members supported recession. One reason was the division of authority between the state and the federal government, which they believed created confusion over what rules applied in each area. The statement also noted that the state of California was not providing the funds necessary to maintain and care for the valley. Roads were few and in poor condition. The number of tourists who visited the valley each year was increasing but there were not enough accommodations for them.

The Sierra Club's statement was printed and distributed to members of the California state legislature. However, several California interest groups still objected to losing control of Yosemite Valley. The club had to plan its strategy carefully. When the California legislature debated the issue, Muir and other members of the club made several trips to Sacramento, the Capital, to talk to committee members and legislators. Muir also enlisted the support of a powerful friend, Edward Harriman, president of the Southern Pacific Railroad. They had met on an expedition to Alaska in 1899. The railroad was a strong lobbying power and Harriman instructed his men to do what they could to further Muir's wishes. All these efforts paid off. The recession bill passed the California state legislature by a vote of 21 to 13, and on June 11, 1906, President Roosevelt signed a bill adding Yosemite Valley to the area protected by the national park.

One Sierra Club board member summarized the importance of this victory:

> The Club is to be congratulated on this happy outcome . . . over the control of the Valley. Our President, Mr. Muir . . . advocated this transfer for more than ten years . . . and it was largely due to his

influence that it was brought about. The Club has never accomplished more important work . . . [8]

The Sierra Club is still active today. It sponsors outings and works to protect wild places so they may be enjoyed for years to come.

Wife and Daughters

At about the same time the club began its political battle for Yosemite Valley, nineteen-year-old Helen Muir developed a serious respiratory illness. When a doctor recommended dry, desert air as the best treatment, Muir and his older daughter Wanda, took Helen to Arizona. However, within a few weeks, Muir was called home. His wife, Louie, had pneumonia and inoperable lung cancer. She died on August 6, 1905.

Saddened by the loss of his wife, Muir returned to Arizona to be with Helen. A letter from Roosevelt encouraged him to "get out among the mountains and the trees as soon as you can. They will do more for you than either man or woman could."[9] After a few months, Muir began to explore the desert. He visited a forest of petrified wood, where mineral deposits had turned a forest of fallen tree trunks into stone. He realized that this remarkable area would soon disappear if left unprotected. Tourists were taking the petrified logs as souvenirs, and a mill was crushing the logs to make an abrasive, a powder used for grinding or polishing. Muir brought this problem to the public's attention and Roosevelt created the Petrified Forest National Monument.

By the end 1906, Helen was well again and Wanda had settled on the Muir Ranch with her new husband, Thomas Hanna. Muir returned to his California home. Though he did not know it, he was about to begin his toughest battle.

THE LAST
STAND

In 1906, John Muir's victory celebration over the recession of Yosemite Valley was cut short when he learned that Yosemite National Park's beautiful Hetch Hetchy Valley was in danger. The city of San Francisco, California, was looking for a cheaper source of water. City leaders wanted to dam the Hetch Hetchy Valley to make a reservoir, and pipe the water into the city. Supporters of this project argued that the valley would not be missed. Muir disagreed. He wrote that the "Hetch Hetchy Valley, far from being a plain, common rock-bound meadow . . . [was] a grand landscaped garden, one of Nature's rarest and most precious mountain temples."[1]

The Hetch Hetchy Valley was described as another Yosemite. Today it is the site of the Hetch Hetchy Reservoir.

The valley was described by those fortunate enough to see it as another Yosemite. A steep cliff much like Yosemite's El Capitain, a rock wall that towered eighteen hundred feet over the valley floor, and Hetch Hetchy Falls, which carried more water than Yosemite Falls, dropped seventeen hundred feet in a series of cascades. Unfortunately, some of its scenic features—steep rocky walls and narrow outlet—also made the Hetch Hetchy very appealing as a natural reservoir. As early as 1901, San Francisco had applied to the secretary of the interior for reservoir rights in two different locations in the Sierras—the Hetch Hetchy Valley and Lake Eleanor. Secretary of the Interior Ethan Allen Hitchcock initially rejected the application. He believed it violated the 1890 law that had created Yosemite National Park. However, in 1901, the Right of Way Act was quietly passed. This act

> authorized the Secretary to grant rights of way through government reservations [National Parks and Forests] for all kinds of canals, ditches, pipes and pipe lines, flumes, tunnels, or other water conduits, and for domestic, public or other beneficial uses.[2]

The act provided the legal grounds for approval of San Francisco's application.

The Great San Francisco Earthquake and Fire

On April 18, 1906, shortly after five in the morning, an earthquake hit San Francisco. Hundreds of people were killed. Electric power lines and gas mains were broken. Many buildings were destroyed, including the Sierra Club office and its records and library.

Fires broke out and burned out of control for several days because of broken water mains. San Franciscans were now more water-conscious than ever. The city doubled its efforts to gain the Hetch Hetchy as a water supply.

The Sierra Club's Battle

Muir did everything he could to preserve the Hetch Hetchy. He wrote letters, sent telegrams, made speeches, gave interviews, and published pamphlets. However, in 1908, the city of San Francisco resubmitted its application for the Hetch Hechy and Lake Eleanor. The newly appointed Secretary of the Interior James R. Garfield issued "a revocable permit"[3] to San Francisco for reservoir rights at both Hetch Hetchy and Lake Eleanor, with the condition that the Lake Eleanor site be developed first.

Since there was a chance that the permit could be cancelled, Muir continued to fight. In 1909, he served as a guide for another presidential visit to Yosemite National Park. President William Howard Taft weighed three hundred pounds and was not an outdoorsman, like former President Theodore Roosevelt. However, the president decided to hike four miles from the top of Glacier Point to the valley floor with Muir. As they walked, Muir voiced his disapproval of the damming of Hetch Hetchy. He also showed Taft plans for roads and trails that would someday link Yosemite Valley, Tuolumne Meadows, and the Hetch Hetchy, allowing more tourists to enjoy the scenic area.

Impressed by Muir's plans, Taft appointed a board of engineers to study the Lake Eleanor site.[4] The report, which stated that Lake Eleanor could supply enough water to meet San Francisco's water needs, provided needed encouragement for Muir and his supporters.[5] The Hetch Hetchy seemed to be safe while Taft remained in office.

However, the controversy sparked by this issue created other problems for the Sierra Club. Many members lived in San Francisco. They believed the dam was necessary and objected to the board of directors' opposition to the project. Muir was frustrated by this conflict, and in 1909, he considered resigning as the club's president.[6] Finally, the directors decided to put the issue of the Hetch Hetchy to a vote of the club's thirteen hundred members. When the results were tallied, 589 members voted to preserve the Hetch Hetchy in its natural state. Only 161 voted in favor of damming the site. Muir decided to stay on as president and the club continued the fight.

More Writing and Travel

While the controversy dragged on, Muir continued to write—slowly—since he refused to send out a carelessly written piece of work. *Stickeen* was published in 1909, *My First Summer in the Sierra* in 1911, followed by *The Yosemite*—a guidebook of the region, and *The Story of My Boyhood and Youth.*

In 1911, Muir took time away from writing to go to South America, a trip he had planned years ago

Muir Woods

While Muir battled to save the Hetch Hetchy Valley, his reputation helped save another wilderness area. William Kent, an outdoorsman who admired Muir's writing, owned a beautiful forested "Redwood Canyon"[7] about fifteen miles from San Francisco. In 1907, the canyon was also considered as a possible site for a reservoir, but Kent wished to preserve the area for its scenic beauty. He campaigned successfully to have the canyon declared a national monument. Though Kent had never met Muir, he requested that the new national monument be given the name Muir Woods.

Today, many visitors take the short trip across Golden Gate Bridge to enjoy the beauty of this redwood forest named in honor of John Muir.

while living in Indianapolis, Indiana. Friends, family, and even his doctor tried to discourage the seventy-three-year-old man from traveling so far alone. However, Muir set sail for South America in August. He traveled up the Amazon River one thousand miles by steamboat, spent a night high in the Andes Mountains in a forest of monkey puzzle trees, an evergreen with branches that intersect to form unusual angles, then sailed on to Africa. At the end of this seven-month adventure, Muir returned home in time to celebrate his seventy-fifth birthday on April 21, 1911.

The Final Showdown

In 1913, the battle for the Hetch Hetchy again heated up when President Woodrow Wilson took office. The new administration appointed Franklin K. Lane as the secretary of the interior. Lane had served as a city attorney for San Francisco. He believed the Hetch Hetchy water was essential for the city. Lane immediately let members of congress know that he supported damming the valley.

Muir summoned all his resources. Editorials and articles supporting the preservationist point of view were published in hundreds of newspapers and in magazines like *Century* and *Atlantic Monthly*. Members of Congress received thousands of letters and telegrams from people who wanted the valley to be preserved. Women's clubs and other organizations added their voices to the protest. Muir now had reason to hope that the Hetch Hetchy was safe, and that the vote would go in favor of the preservationists. As the final showdown drew near, he wrote to his daughter Helen, "I'll be relieved when it's settled, for it's killing me."[8]

Unfortunately, all Muir's efforts, all the newspaper editorials and telegrams, and all the protests of the Sierra Club and other organizations were not enough. On December 6, 1913, when the issue finally came to a vote, forty-three senators voted in favor of giving the City of San Francisco permission to flood the Hetch Hetchy Valley. Only twenty-five opposed the damming. The loss of this beautiful valley, supposedly a protected area within a national park, was a major defeat for Muir. He summed up his feelings in one letter, saying that "wrong prevailed over the best aroused sentiment of the entire country."[9]

However, some good did come from this great disappointment. Public awareness had been stirred and no violation as destructive as the damming of the Hetch Hetchy has happened again in a national park.

Final Days

Muir sadly began work revising his journals for his next book, *Travels in Alaska,* but made little progress.[10] He was exhausted after the long struggle for the Hetch Hetchy. He had an infection in his right lung and a chronic cough. As he tried to regain his strength, Muir took great pleasure in the "boy undergrowth," as he fondly called his grandsons.[11] He often set his pen aside to play with Wanda's sons, Strentzel, John, Richard, and to hold her fourth son, Robert, who was born in August 1913. The family lived near him on the ranch. His younger daughter, Helen, also had two sons—Muir and Stanley. She had married Buell A. Funk in 1910. They lived on a cattle ranch in Daggett, California about four hundred miles south of Martinez.

Finally, Muir's health improved enough to allow him to keep a regular writing schedule. He usually began work by seven in the morning and often did not quit until after ten at night. He made steady progress on his book with the help of a typist, although occasionally the infected lung slowed his progress.

In June 1914, Helen's third son, John, was born. Muir wanted to see his new grandchild, but decided to wait until his *Travels in Alaska* was nearly completed.[12] In the middle of December, he packed a suitcase and boarded the train for Daggett. He took along his Alaska manuscript. He planned to revise it once more during his stay with Helen.

Muir took great pleasure in the "boy undergrowth," as he fondly called his grandsons. He often set his pen aside to play with Wanda's sons, Strentzel, John, and Richard.

The weather was cold and windy when Muir arrived in Daggett shortly after two in the morning. Before he reached the Funk ranch, Muir began to feel ill. By evening his condition had grown worse and Helen called the doctor. Muir's ailment was diagnosed as pneumonia. He was taken immediately by train to a hospital in Los Angeles. The next morning, he seemed to improve, but by the end of the day—Christmas Eve—all John Muir's tramping came to an end. With the manuscript pages of his last book, *Travels in Alaska*, spread about him, seventy-six-year-old John Muir died.

John Muir's Namesake

The grandson that John Muir saw for the first time a few days before his death would become his namesake years later. In 1934, after her husband, Buell Funk, was killed in an automobile accident, Helen legally changed her last name and the names of her three youngest children, Stanley, John, and Walter, back to Muir. Her oldest son, whose first name was Muir, kept the name Funk. Helen's son John, who was born a few months before his grandfather died, was then known as John Muir.

Friends suggested that Yosemite Valley was the only appropriate place for his grave. However, Muir had once told his daughter Wanda that he wished to be buried next to his wife, Louie. The family respected his wish. John Muir was laid to rest in the Strentzel family cemetery near Martinez, California.

10

A LIVING LEGACY

Today, we can still learn about John Muir's fight for wilderness preservation by reading his own words. Presidents, congressmen, and American citizens were moved by the power of words like these:

> Any fool can destroy trees. They cannot run away; and if they could, they would still be destroyed—chased and hunted down as long as fun or a dollar could be got out of their bark hides, branching horns, or magnificent bole [tree trunk] backbones . . . Through all the wonderful, eventful centuries . . . God has cared for these trees . . . but he cannot save them from fools—only Uncle Sam can do that.[1]

Muir's powerful writing had influenced President Grover Cleveland to establish thirteen forest reserves. His message persuaded President

Theodore Roosevelt to add 148 million acres to the reserves, and to create five national parks and twenty-three national monuments. Some historians even honor Muir as the "Father of our National Parks." In 1916, less than two years after his death, the United States Congress created the national park service to protect and manage the wilderness Muir helped to preserve. Each year, millions of Americans who visit Yosemite, Sequoia, Mount Ranier, the Petrified Forest, and Grand Canyon National Parks appreciate the power of John Muir's pen.

His Last Book

The book John Muir was editing when he died, *Travels in Alaska*, was published in 1915, after a friend finished the typing and editing of the manuscript. In the years since, his essays, letters, and journals have been published again and again.

Muir's poetic writing style has introduced many to the wonders of nature. "Never was there a naturalist who could hold his [audience] so well," noted a journalist friend, "and none had so much to tell."[2] Even today new collections and editions appear regularly, making it possible for John Muir's voice to continue the defense of the wilderness.

The Conservation Movement

The last half of Muir's life was dedicated to the preservation of what he considered irreplaceable national treasures—some of the most beautiful mountains and forests in the United States. In the mid-1870s, when Muir first began to write and lobby for wilderness conservation, logging companies commonly stripped entire mountainsides of trees. Herds of sheep and cattle often overgrazed meadows, killing vegetation by eating the entire plant, even the roots. Miners regularly destroyed cliffs and hillsides in their search for gold, silver, and other valuable minerals. In general, Americans believed that the wilderness was there to be used—when one forest, meadow, or mountain was destroyed, there was always another a little farther away.

However, Muir realized that these natural resources were not limitless. If such wasteful practices were not checked, the wilderness would be lost forever. His ideas represented the beginning of the American conservation movement, a radical new concept in land use. He believed that wild places needed to be preserved for future generations, and his efforts to defend these natural resources were quite successful. By the time of his death in 1914, most Americans were committed to using the country's natural resources more wisely.

The John Muir Trail

In 1916, the Sierra Club successfully lobbied the California legislature for ten thousand dollars to begin construction on the John Muir Trail. The 210-mile project was completed more than twenty years later, in 1938.

Today, adventuresome hikers trek along this wilderness trail that begins in Yosemite Valley and climbs steeply alongside Vernal and Nevada falls to Little Yosemite Valley. From there, the trail goes over Cathedral Pass to Tuolumne Meadows. As they venture on, hikers enjoy spectacular views of Mount Lyell, the highest peak in Yosemite National Park, and of the large glacier on its north slope, Lyell Glacier.

The John Muir Trail continues on through some of the finest mountain scenery in the Sierra Nevada range until it reaches its ends at the summit of Mount Whitney, the highest point in the continental United States. No other tribute could be more appropriate for the Sierra Club's first president. These meadows, canyons, and mountains held a special place in Muir's heart.

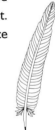

Muir's influence continues to live through the modern conservation movement. Today, the Sierra Club is only one of many organizations that actively work to protect the environment. Others such as the Wilderness Society, the Defenders of Wildlife, and the Nature Conservancy fight to preserve the forests and other wild places. Largely due to the work of these groups, millions of acres are now protected under the United States Wilderness Act that was passed in 1964.

The importance of ecology (how people effect the world they live in) and environmental studies is also widely recognized. Kindergarten and elementary students are introduced to the basics of how to care for our earth and its natural resources. Colleges and universities offer courses that teach students about the relationships between man and his environment—relationships that Muir observed and valued over a hundred years ago.

The importance of John Muir's role in the American conservation movement has not been forgotten. In 1965, *Time* magazine named him "the real father of conservation."[3] He was also the second member named to the Conservation Hall of Fame sponsored by the Wildlife Federation. Theodore Roosevelt was the first.

Other Memorials

In 1959, the John Muir Memorial Association was founded. Its purpose was to preserve

> the memory of John Muir and his contributions to mankind, to apply his principles to the conservation of our natural resources . . . to educate children and adults in the love of nature, [and] to preserve and protect the forest, streams, and mountains of America.[4]

It was also through the efforts of this organization that John Muir's home in Martinez, California, was declared a National Historic Site in 1964. Eventually, the United States government purchased the surrounding 325 acres, adding the hills where Muir roamed with his daughters, Helen and Wanda, to the site.

In 1976, members of the California Historical Society voted Muir the greatest Californian in the state's history. John Muir Day is celebrated each year on his birthday, April 21, in the state of California. In 1964 and again in 1998, the United States Postal Service issued commemorative stamps honoring Muir.

His fame has also stretched back across the Atlantic Ocean to his birthplace. Today in Dunbar, Scotland, tourists can visit the John Muir County Park and the John Muir Birthplace Museum.

John Muir's home in Martinez, California, was declared a National Historic Site in 1964.

In addition, Scottish wildlands are being protected through the efforts of the John Muir Trust.

Living Legacy

The greatest memorial of all to the naturalist and author is Yosemite National Park. The park, whose boundaries Muir himself drew, covers a large scenic area of the Sierra Nevada Mountains. Within the park, visitors can explore the high alpine wilderness of Tuolumne Meadows, the groves of giant sequoias, and Yosemite Valley.

Though two hundred miles of roads allow visitors to see all these areas by car, to get to know the Yosemite that Muir loved, it is necessary to take a few steps along a trail. There are many paths from which to chose. Take a gentle walk along the edge of the peaceful Merced River, where Muir built his first home in the valley.

John Muir's spirit lives on in his own words: "Climb the mountains and get their good tidings. Nature's peace will flow into you as sunshine flows into trees. The winds will blow their energy, while cares will drop off like autumn leaves."

Climb the steep trail to the very top of Yosemite Falls and share Muir's excitement of watching the water begins its sixteen-hundred-foot plunge to the valley. Or truly follow in Muir's footsteps—pack a few necessary provisions and tramp out into the wilderness along the John Muir Trail.

Whichever path a visitor chooses, he or she will quickly be surrounded by breathtaking grandeur, that, for the most part, only nature has changed over the last hundred years. For that, we can thank John Muir and his dedication to the preservation of America's wild places.

CHRONOLOGY

1838—Born in Dunbar, Scotland, on April 21.

1849—Family immigrates to Wisconsin.

1854—Constructs inventions.

1856—Family moves from Fountain Lake to Hickory Hill.

1860—Leaves home to exhibit inventions in Madison, Wisconsin; Meets Jeanne Carr, wife of Ezra Carr, a professor at the University of Wisconsin.

1861—Enrolls at the University of Wisconsin and attends classes for two-and-a-half years; Learns about geology and invents a study desk.

1862—Becomes interested in botany.

1864—Travels to Canada.

1866—Moves to Indianapolis, Indiana.

1867—Temporarily blinded in a factory accident; When his sight returns after a month, decides to leave work to study nature; Sets out on one-thousand-mile walk in September.

1868—Visits Yosemite for the first time in April.

1869—Begins studies of the Sierras.

1870—Works in Yosemite at Hutchings' sawmill; Makes first visit to Hetch Hetchy Valley.

1871—Ralph Waldo Emerson visits in April; Article "Yosemite Glaciers" is published in December.

1873—Spends winter in Oakland, California; Writes series of articles on Yosemite.

1874—Climbs Mount Shasta in April; "Studies in the Sierra," is published by *Overland Monthly*; Jeanne Carr introduces Muir to Louie Wanda Strentzel.

1876—Article "God's First Temples," urging government protection of trees, is published in April; Gives first public lecture.

1878—Begins contact with the Strentzel family.

1879—Gets engaged to Louie Wanda Strentzel; Makes first trip to Alaska; Discovers Glacier Bay and Muir Glacier while traveling with S. Hall Young.

1880—Marries Louie Strentzel on April 14; Makes second trip to Alaska and has adventure with Stickeen.

1881—Makes third trip to Alaska; First daughter, Wanda, is born on March 25.

1882—Becomes a rancher and fruit farmer for eight years.

1885—Daniel Muir dies, John is at his bedside.

1886—Second daughter, Helen, is born on January 23.

1888—*Picturesque California* is published.

1890—Makes fourth trip to Alaska; Articles lobbying for Yosemite National Park are published in *Century Magazine*; Yosemite becomes a national park.

1892—Helps found the Sierra Club and is elected its first president.

1894—*The Mountains of California* is published.

1896—Joins the United States Forestry Commission; Mother, Ann Gilrye Muir, dies on June 23.

1897—Articles on forest preservation published in *Harper's Weekly* and *Atlantic Monthly*.

1901—*Our National Parks* is published in April.

1903—Camps in Yosemite with President Theodore Roosevelt; Starts world tour.

1905—Begins battle to have Yosemite Valley returned to federal control; Wife, Louie Muir, dies on August 6; Discovers Petrified Forest in Arizona.

1906—Yosemite Valley becomes part of Yosemite National Park.

1907—Begins fight for the Hetch Hetchy Valley.

1909—*Stickeen* is published; Escorts President William Taft through Yosemite Valley.

1911—*My First Summer in the Sierra* is published; Makes year-long trip to South America and Africa.

1912—*Yosemite* is published.

1913—The battle for the Hetch Hetchy is lost; *Story of My Boyhood and Youth* is published.

1914—Dies in Los Angeles on December 24.

1915—*Travels in Alaska* is published.

CHAPTER NOTES

Chapter 1. "An Adventure with a Dog and a Glacier"

1. John Muir, *Stickeen: A Story of a Dog*, (Chester, Conn.: Applewood Books, n.d.), p. 37.

2. Ibid., p. 47.

3. Ibid., p. 48.

4. Ibid., p. 58.

5. Ibid., p. 53.

6. Ibid., p. 54.

7. Ibid., p. 63.

8. Thurman Wilkins, *John Muir: Apostle of Nature* (Norman: University of Oklahoma Press, 1995), p. 150.

9. Muir., p. 65.

10. Ibid., pp. 66–67.

Chapter 2. Scottish Castles and Bairns

1. James Mitchell Clarke, *The Life and Adventures of John Muir*, (San Diego: The Word Shop, Inc., 1979), p. 3.

2. John Muir, *The Story of My Boyhood and Youth* (Madison: University of Wisconsin Press, 1965), p. 4.

3. Clarke, p. 3.

4. Ibid., p. 6.

5. Terry Gifford, ed., *John Muir, His Life and Letters and Other Writings* (Seattle: Mountaineers Books, 1996), p. 19.

6. Ibid., p. 21.

7. Clarke, p. 5.

8. Frederick Turner, *Rediscovering America: John Muir in His Time and Ours* (New York: Viking, 1985), p. 16.

9. Clarke, p. 5.

10. Ibid.

11. Muir, p. 20.

12. Clarke, p. 6.

13. Stephen Fox, *John Muir and his Legacy: the American Conservation Movement* (Boston: Little, Brown and Company, 1981), p. 29.

14. Muir, pp. 43–44.

15. Muir, p. 45.

16. Ibid.

17. Ibid.

18. Ibid, p. 46.

19. Clarke, p. 9.

Chapter 3. A Whole New World

1. John Muir, *The Story of My Boyhood and Youth* (Madison: University of Wisconsin Press, 1965), p. 53.

2. James Mitchell Clarke, *The Life and Adventures of John Muir* (San Diego: The Word Shop, Inc., 1979), p. 15.

3. Muir, p. 163.

4. Terry Gifford, ed., *John Muir, His Life and Letters and Other Writings* (Seattle: Mountaineers Books, 1996), p. 38.

5. Muir, pp. 82–83.

6. Ibid., p. 87.

7. Stephen Fox, *John Muir and his Legacy: the American Conservation Movement* (Boston: Little, Brown and Company, 1981), p. 33.

8. Ibid., p. 32.

9. Clarke, p. 21.

10. Muir, p. 195.

11. Ibid.

12. Ibid.

13. Ibid., p. 198.

14. Clarke, p. 24.

15. Ibid., p. 27.

Chapter 4. Inventor, Student, and Botanist

1. Frederick Turner, *Rediscovering America: John Muir in His Time and Ours* (New York: Viking, 1985), p. 84.

2. Ibid.

3. John Muir, *The Story of My Boyhood and Youth* (Madison: University of Wisconsin Press, 1965), pp. 283–284.

4. Turner, p. 98.

5. Ibid., p. 91.

6. Ibid., p. 106.

7. Ibid., pp. 101–102.

8. Terry Gifford, ed., *John Muir: His Life and Letters and Other Writings* (Seattle: Mountaineers Books, 1996), pp. 70–71.

9. Ibid.

10. Turner, p. 125.

11. Thurman Wilkins, *John Muir: Apostle of Nature* (Norman: University of Oklahoma Press, 1995), p. 45.

Chapter 5. Road to Yosemite

1. John Earl, *John Muir's Longest Walk* (New York: Doubleday & Company, Inc, 1975), p. 29.

2. Ibid., p. 44.

3. Ibid., p. 82.

4. Frederick Turner, *Rediscovering America: John Muir in His Time and Ours* (New York: Viking, 1985), pp. 162–163.

5. Thurman Wilkins, *John Muir: Apostle of Nature* (Norman: University of Oklahoma Press, 1995), p. 58.

6. Ibid., p. 64.

7. James Mitchell Clarke, *The Life and Adventures of John Muir* (San Diego: The Word Shop, Inc., 1979), p. 68.

8. Edwin Way Teal, *The Wilderness World of John Muir* (Boston: Houghton Mifflin Company, 1954) pp. 126–127.

9. Linnie Marsh Wolfe, *Son of the Wilderness* (New York: Alfred A. Knopf, 1946), p. 121.

10. Ibid., p. 71.

11. Teal, p. 162.

12. N. King Huber, *The Geological Story of Yosemite National Park* (Yosemite National Park, Calif.: Yosemite Association, 1989), p. 1.

13. Ibid.

14. Lee Stetson, ed. *The Wild Muir: Twenty-two of John Muir's Greatest Adventures* (Yosemite National Park, Calif.: Yosemite Association, 1994), p. 74.

15. Clarke, p. 99.

Chapter 6. Scientist, Author, and Explorer

1. James Mitchell Clarke, *The Life and Adventures of John Muir* (San Diego: The Word Shop, Inc., 1979), p. 90.

2. Terry Gifford, ed., *John Muir: His Life and Letters and Other Writings* (Seattle: Mountaineers Books, 1996), p. 199.

3. Frederick Turner, *Rediscovering America: John Muir in His Time and Ours* (New York: Viking, 1985), p. 227.

4. Gifford, p. 208.

5. Turner, p. 235.

6. Lee Stetson, ed. *The Wild Muir: Twenty-two of John Muir's Greatest Adventures* (Yosemite National Park, Calif.: Yosemite Association, 1994), p. 112.

7. Ibid., pp. 112–113.

8. Ibid., pp. 250–251.

9. Ibid., p. 255.

10. Gifford, p. 199.

11. Ibid., p. 210.

Chapter 7. Family Ties

1. Terry Gifford, ed., *John Muir, His Life and Letters and Other Writings* (Seattle: Mountaineers Books, 1996), p. 253.

2. Ibid.

3. Frederick Turner, *Rediscovering America: John Muir in His Time and Ours* (New York: Viking, 1985), p. 263.

4. Ibid., p. 259.

5. Ibid., p. 253.

6. Ibid., p. 4.

7. John Muir, *Travels in Alaska* (San Francisco: Sierra Club Books, 1988.), p. 191.

8. Ibid., p. 205.

9. Thurman Wilkins, *John Muir: Apostle of Nature* (Norman: University of Oklahoma Press, 1995), p. 149.

10. James Mitchell Clarke, *The Life and Adventures of John Muir* (San Diego: The Word Shop, Inc., 1979), p. 226.

11. Ibid., p. 150.

12. Linnie Marsh Wolfe, *The Life of John Muir* (Madison: The University of Wisconsin Press, 1945), p. 227.

13. Gifford p. 279.

14. Ibid., pp. 282–283.

15. Wolfe, p. 255.

16. Gifford, p. 289.

Chapter 8. Crusading for the Wilderness

1. Terry Gifford, ed., *John Muir, His Life and Letters and Other Writings* (Seattle: Mountaineers Books, 1996), p. 305.

2. Ibid., p. 306.

3. Ibid., p. 320.

4. Ibid., p. 328.

5. Ibid., p. 333.

6. Ibid., p. 374.

7. Holway R. Jones, *John Muir and the Sierra Club: The Battle for Yosemite* (San Fransisco: Sierra Club, 1965), p. 305.

8. Michael P. Cohen, *The Pathless Way: John Muir and American Wilderness* (Madison: University of Wisconsin Press, 1984), p. 78.

9. Gifford, p. 348.

Chapter 9. The Last Stand

1. Thurman Wilkins, *John Muir: Apostle of Nature* (Norman: University of Oklahoma Press, 1995), p. 227.

2. Ibid.

3. Ibid., p. 128.

4. Ibid., p. 233.

5. Ibid.

6. Ibid., p. 234.

7. James Mitchell Clarke, *The Life and Adventures of John Muir* (San Diego: The Word Shop, Inc., 1979), p. 304.

8. Wilkins, p. 240.

9. Terry Gifford, ed., *John Muir, His Life and Letters and Other Writings* (Seattle: Mountaineers Books, 1996), p. 380.

10. Ibid., p. 365.

11. Wilkins, p. 248.

12. Ibid., p. 250.

Chapter 10. A Living Legacy

1. John Muir, *Our National Parks* (Madison: University of Madison Press, 1981), pp. 264–265.

2. Thurman Wilkins, *John Muir: Apostle of Nature* (Norman: University of Oklahoma Press, 1995), p. 243.

3. Ibid., p. 253.

4. "Chronology of the Life and Legacy of John Muir, From his birth to present day," *The Life and Contributions of John Muir*, 2000, <http://www.sierraclub.org/john_muir_exhibit> (October 2, 2001).

GLOSSARY

abyss—A deep crack in the surface of a glacier; a crevasse.

bairn—Scottish word for child.

barometer—An instrument for measuring atmospheric pressure.

botany—The science that deals with plant life.

choke damp—A suffocating gas mixture of carbon monoxide and nitrogen often found in mines.

chronic—Lasting a long time or recurring often.

conservation—The official care and protection of natural resources.

crevasse—A deep crack in a glacier.

fiord—A narrow arm of the sea bordered by steep cliffs.

frostbite—An injury to the tissues of the body by exposure to intense cold.

locust—A grasshopper-like insect that often travels in large swarms and destroys nearly all the vegetation in its path.

malaria—A disease transmitted by mosquitoes; symptoms include severe chills and fever.

naturalist—A person who studies nature by direct observation.

ornithologist—A person who studies birds.

premonition—A feeling that something specific is going to happen.

preservationist—A person who wishes to take action to preserve something.

FURTHER READING

Books

Brimner, Larry Dane, *Glaciers*. Chicago: Children's Press, 2000.

Halvorsen, Lisa. *Letters Home from Yosemite*. Woodbridge, Conn.: Blackbirch Marketing, 2000.

Ito, Tom. *John Muir*. San Diego: Lucent Books, 1996.

Maruca, Mary. *A Kid's Guide to Exploring John Muir*. Tucson: Western National Parks Association, 1999.

Rubay, Donnell. *Stickeen: John Muir and the Brave Little Dog*. Nevada City, Calif.: Dawn Publishers, 1998.

Schuman, Michael A., *Theodore Roosevelt*. Springfield, N.J.: Enslow Publishers, Inc., 1997.

Stanley, Phyllis M., *American Environmental Heroes*. Springfield, N.J.: Enslow Publishers, Inc., 1997.

Internet Addresses

National Park Service. "History." *Muir Woods National Monument*. March 12, 2001. <http://www.nps.gov/muwo/history/history.htm>.

National Park Service. "History." *Yosemite National Park*. October 2, 2001. <http://www.nps.gov/yose/nature/history.htm>.

National Park Service. "John Muir National Historical Site." September 20, 2001. <http://www.nps.gov/jomu/>.

Sierra Club. "John Muir Exhibit." 2001. <http://www.sierraclub.org/john_muir_exhibit>.

INDEX